MW00452115

Berkshire Ghosts, Legends, and Lore

E. Ashley Rooney

*Photos by D. Peter Lund
unless otherwise noted*

Schiffer Publishing Ltd®

4880 Lower Valley Road, Atglen, Pennsylvania 19310

Schiffer Books are available at special discounts for bulk purchases for sales promotions or premiums. Special editions, including personalized covers, corporate imprints, and excerpts can be created in large quantities for special needs. For more information contact the publisher:

Published by Schiffer Publishing Ltd.
4880 Lower Valley Road
Atglen, PA 19310
Phone: (610) 593-1777; Fax: (610) 593-2002
E-mail: Info@schifferbooks.com

For the largest selection of fine reference books on this and related subjects, please visit our web site at **www.schifferbooks.com**
We are always looking for people to write books on new and related subjects. If you have an idea for a book please contact us at the above address.

This book may be purchased from the publisher.
Include $3.95 for shipping.
Please try your bookstore first.
You may write for a free catalog.

In Europe, Schiffer books are distributed by
Bushwood Books
6 Marksbury Ave.
Kew Gardens
Surrey TW9 4JF England
Phone: 44 (0) 20 8392-8585; Fax: 44 (0) 20 8392-9876
E-mail: info@bushwoodbooks.co.uk
Website: www.bushwoodbooks.co.uk
Free postage in the U.K., Europe; air mail at cost.

Other Schiffer Books on Related Subjects
Ghosts of Valley Forge and Phoenixville, 978-0-7643-2633-2, $14.95
See catalogue for information about Schiffer Publishing's paranormal department, featuring ghostly tales from many states and regions.

Designed by Mark David Bowyer
Type set in Buffied / Lydian BT / Korinna BT

ISBN: 978-0-7643-2797-1
Printed in China

Contents

Acknowledgments

Hunting for ghosts and the legends of the past is an interesting challenge. The enthusiasm of Paul Oleskiewicz, of the Berkshire Paranormal Group, played a major role in the creation of this book, as did the companionship of Sam and Lee Evans on one ghost-hunting trip, and the commitment of my husband, D. Peter Lund.

NOTE: Many of us don't quite understand ghosts. In this book, I have told or retold these stories from a fictional perspective, trying from my comfortable place to make sense of the past. These lost voices must continue to be heard; their untold stories must continue to be recounted. For they represent the ones who didn't live to tell their stories themselves.

Introduction

The Mohegans were the first inhabitants of the Berkshires, and by the time the Dutch and English arrived around 1730, they were living in small villages in the Stockbridge and Sheffield regions. In theory, the English settlers believed in befriending and converting the Indians to Christianity. In practice, many of the settlers considered the Indians to be "pernicious vermin," wanting only to get rid of them. The first missionary to Stockbridge was Rev. John Sergeant, who built his Mission House in 1739; it's now a historic site on Main Street. Sergeant had great hopes for a new society.

In 1774, the County Congress or the Berkshire Convention met at the Stockbridge Tavern under the sign of the red lion with the green tail (now the famous Red Lion Inn on Main Street). With Mark Hopkins and Theodore Sedgwick presiding, they voted not to consume any British manufactured goods. It was one of the first such formal actions in the colonies.

There was industry in the Berkshires towards the north, but the Berkshires are world renown for the charming valley villages of Stockbridge and Lenox. In the early nineteenth century, Stockbridge, a rural farming community, was on a main route of the stagecoach line between Boston and Albany; each day four coaches made regular stops going each direction. Over the years, it became the home of authors and the first families;

Lenox developed soon after the Civil War. According to Cleveland Amory, Lenox had thirty-five cottages in 1880 and seventy-five by 1900 *(p. 21)*.

The villages were discovered, however, once the railroad chugged into town. Captivated by the beauty of the Berkshires and the geographical ease of reaching it, wealthy New Yorkers and Bostonians would pack up their families, their household necessities, luggage, horses, and carriages and travel to Lenox via the New York, New Haven and Hartford Railroad. The developer of the New York City transit system and Cleveland's Secretary of the Navy, William C. Whitney, even transported deer, elk, moose, antelope, bison, and other exotic beasts to his summer home and game preserve on October Mountain.

Once there, they established their domiciles, which they blithely called cottages, an incongruous term for these Tudor castles, Swiss chalets and other grand villas. Massive in size — one had one hundred rooms, another, ninety-four — these cottages were set on gargantuan estates and were centers of activity. Although the summer people often brought their servants, who were frequently new immigrants, they also employed the local people during their stay. The villagers worked in the gardens, the greenhouses, and the farms, foregoing their usual hardscrabble existence for the brief time that the cottagers were in residence,

From the late 1800s to 1920, a period often called the Gilded Age, the Berkshires were a summer colony for the American economic elite or the American "aristocracy" of the time. These tiny villages (Lenox had a population of 1,845 and Stockbridge, 2,089) played host to the most powerful people of the age. Their decisions affected American society, politics, and law. The bankers, the heads of industry, the robber barons—they were the ones with the next daring idea, the next new product, and the next great invention that would help transform the country to an industrialized nation of international standing. The rest of society was watching and eventually emulating.

The villages already had a reputation as a home for authors, painters, poets, and clergy. Writers such as Longfellow, Hawthorne, Melville, Henry James, and Edith Wharton, and artists such as Norman Rockwell and Daniel Chester French, found their home here. The list goes on and on. During the Gilded Age, a list of their cottages and their guests read like the index of the brightest and the best of that century from Andrew Carnegie, to George Westinghouse, to Harry Payne Whitney. Then there were the presidents, royalty, diplomats, and bankers.

They all took their leisure very seriously. They came to go to the hunt, the gymkhanas, and the tetherball tournaments; to attend the house parties, the balls, and horse shows; to play golf, tennis, and croquet; to dance, to dine, and to flirt. They came to compete, to impress, and to enjoy this life of luxury.

Over the generations, some estates became inns and resort hotels, responding to the increase in tourism. Others became private schools, religious institutions, and health centers. Once the Boston Symphony Orchestra made its summer home at Tanglewood, the Berkshires' reputation as a region that combined music, theater, dance, and art with natural beauty thrived again.

The Berkshire Hills are a wide rolling plateau, consuming some twenty miles, in western Massachusetts. The region is only forty-nine miles long from north to south, extending entirely from Connecticut to Vermont. In breadth, it varies from twenty-four miles to twelve at its narrowest point. The area encompasses approximately one thousand square miles of forests, fields, hills, rivers and lakes; the latter form the headwaters of several rivers.

This beautiful area is also the home of many ghosts, legends, and folk stories. Some of these stories descended from the natives; many came from the time of the American Revolution; others came from those who lived in the famous cottages during the Gilded Age. These restless spirits, or paranormal manifestations, make a visit to Berkshires all that much richer.

Part One:

Ghosts of the Berkshires

Many of us have had the hair at the nape of our neck prickle uneasily when we have heard the creak of a stair or felt a sudden chill run down our spine. In the Berkshires, these uneasy feelings happen frequently — for the region has many ghosts…

Although the Indians who once roamed these luminous green valleys and low wooded mountains are long gone, their stories – and their ghosts – still endure…

Then there are the settlers of the area. With their insatiable appetite for territorial expansion, the colonists rapidly pushed westward into the Berkshires, where they acquired land and established frontier communities. They took saws and axes to the wilderness, cutting down the great forests, planting fields, and establishing themselves as farmers on land purchased or taken from the Indians. They too left their ghosts…

The nineteenth century millionaires, who built great summer cottages where they and their staff could retire in unabashed opulence for six weeks during the heat of the summer, followed them. Many ghostly residents still wander about these elegant old mansions…

In fact, while having dinner at one of the more renown resorts, we were regaled with the story of Christina, a mischievous ghost, who threw books, closed cabinets, and remade beds much to the bemusement of the resort's guests. Often the stories of these ghosts are not known—the ghosts are just…present. These ghostly tales endeavor to give these spirits a past and perhaps even a future.

Ghost of Tanglewood

Generally, Boston businessman, Samuel G. Ward, is credited as the first man to assemble tracts of land to form a large Berkshire estate in the early 1840s. Several years later, William Tappan bought a large tract of property adjacent to Ward's. This purchase had significant impact for the future.

Caroline had been coming to visit friends in the Berkshires for years. She reveled in the lush greenness of the meadows, the luxuriant trees, and the lovely small villages. One morning at breakfast soon after they were married, she urged her husband, a Boston merchant and banker, to consider buying a country home.

"William," she said, "we must have a place to retreat to during the hot months. Boston 's air can be so noxious."

"Well, my dear, we have just married…"

"Think," she interjected. "We can get away from the crowded streets and all those evil smells. It would be lovely."

William rattled his paper. "A country home is a big commitment to assume when my career in the bank is just beginning."

She handed him a buttered piece of toast. "You are already doing quite well, William. And, the air and the water are certainly nicer out there."

"Caroline…"

"And so many of our friends go."

Tanglewood is famous worldwide for its music. A music-loving ghost is also thought to haunt the premises.

So they began house hunting along the placid Housatonic River that reflected the gentle green hills. One spring day in 1849, when the trees were in chartreuse leaf, birds sang in every tree, and pink blossoms were lush on the apple trees, they found a small red farmhouse sitting on 210 acres of broad farmland with a long sloping hill down to the shore of Lake Makeenac.

Caroline happily furnished the farmhouse with some precious antiques from William's family, her needlepoint hangings, and braided rugs. She found a local handyman and directed him to plant a garden with hydrangeas, brilliant pink phlox, pink and blue sweet peas, and blue salvia. Near sunset, she would sit on the door stoop and delight in their colors against the purpling Berkshire Hills and the setting sun.

William liked to study the stars in the Berkshires. At first, she found it quite romantic when they would stand outside, arm in arm, looking at the sky. "Star Light, star bright. Grant me my wish tonight," she would chant. "What should I wish for, William?"

"See, Caroline, there's the North Star."

"Where?"

"Right there at the end of the handle of the Little Dipper," he gestured. "See over there."

"I think I want to wish for a rose garden."

"Do you know that many mariners throughout history have used the North Star to stir their course?"

"Hmm… Maybe we could have a picnic tomorrow. We could pack deviled eggs, and I could take those meringues. What do you think?" It was springtime. She had never noticed a season particularly before, but this year the sun was so bright, the birds so loud that she awoke at dawn.

He would watch the movements of the stars and take notes in his journal. Neptune had just been discovered in 1846, and he was hoping, although he knew he was being foolish, that maybe he could discover a new celestial body on his own. Instead, he tried to be content when he spotted Mars or Venus.

Often Caroline would busy herself with cutting flowers or dusting the pictures while William read. But then she would knock at the door and ask when he would be ready to join her for a walk. Engrossed in his book, he would say, "Later, later." When she would return in an hour, he would sigh, light his pipe, and, if she stood at the door long enough, he would get up, grumbling.

On cool June evenings, they would sit in the small parlor after supper. He would read, and she would chatter about the new styles, people she had met at church, or the flowers in her garden. He would look up occasionally and grunt "um" or "yes dear" or "if you say so." Often she would wail, "But William, you aren't listening to me."

On warm, muggy summer evenings, they would sit outside. She would do her needlework. He would put his head back and marvel at the beauty of the heavens. "This is wonderful."

"Yes, it is, dear. If only we had a bigger house, then we could ask our friends to join us and see how truly lovely it is."

"Here, I can see the sun, the moon, the stars, and even the constellations."

"If we just had more rooms and a better looking house…"

"Just think, dear, the vastness of the heavens lies over our heads."

"Then, if we have more room perhaps the Bachelors will join us out here."

Determined to be a good wife, she would make William soft-boiled eggs and toast for breakfast. He would then go to his "study," and she would supervise the staff in cleaning up. Promptly at four in the afternoon, she would serve him Earl Grey tea in a pot with a jug of hot water along side, and small tasteless cookies. He would pull out his newspaper; she would sit and smile. Sometimes, they would walk their land, hand-in-hand. She would point out her flowers, sniffing happily, and pick pink and blue bouquets. He would nod absent-mindedly. At night, William and she would lie in bed and watch the shadows play across the ceiling as the large apple tree outside their window danced in the wind.

Sometimes, he would join her at sunset. She would wrap her arms around him, saying, "How wonderful that you left your work to join me."

"I thought that the night was so clear I might see Venus."

"Oh."

"You know Venus has been known forever. It is the brightest object in the sky except for the sun and the moon. Sometimes people refer to it as the 'morning star' or the 'evening star' because it is so bright."

On her way inside, she sang, "Twinkle, Twinkle, little star, how I wonder where you are."

Caroline's love for landscaping and flowers grew. Her nails chipped and her nose reddened in the sun as she worked with her gardener to plant yellow and pink day lilies for July and red and pink asters for August. The colors of her garden rivaled the rainbow.

One evening, William tried to teach Caroline how to find Orion, but she just threw up her hands.

"I don't want to find the three stars that make up his belt, William."

"But it is quite easy, dear."

"Not for me," she wailed.

"But you don't try," William snapped. Then he relented. "How about the Big Dipper? You can easily see its handle if you look right here."

"Yes, I guess. Who would you like to ask for dinner tomorrow?"

He sighed. "I was hoping we could have a quiet evening at home."

"So you could look at the stars again?" she asked pertly and walked inside.

Their friends, Sam and Anna Ward, lived next door at Highwood, a grand new house designed by Richard Upjohn. Caroline was somewhat jealous. She really wanted Upjohn to design her a new home. She had admired his Trinity Church in New York City. Originally from England, he was said to be responsible for the popularity of the new Gothic Revival style.

William said, "I'm sorry, my dear. We don't need a new house."

"You just want to stay in this little red farmhouse?" she accused.

"Well, I like it. It's comfortable. I can do my work here."

"But William…"

The Tenant of the Red Cottage

Finally, William agreed to rent Highwood from the Wards, who had to return to Boston. He also purchased the vacant property adjacent to Mr. Ward's. William and Caroline offered the red cottage to their friends, Sophia and Nathaniel Hawthorne, a struggling novelist who had recently lost his day job at the Salem Customs House.

From May 1850 until November 1851, Nathaniel Hawthorne and his family lived in the little red farmhouse on the edge of the 210-acre estate, later to be known as Tanglewood. Hawthorne wrote, "There is a glen between this house and the lake through which winds a little brook with pools, and tiny waterfalls over the great roots of trees . . . Beyond the lake is Monument Mountain, looking like a headless sphinx wrapped in a Persian shawl, when clad in the rich and diversified autumnal foliage of its woods." *(Passages from the American Notebooks, Vol. 2)*

Hawthorne worked in the farmhouse's attic, where he could see the lake. There, he wrote *The House of the Seven Gables* and began his *Wonder Book* and *Tanglewood Tales*, a re-writing of a number of Greek myths for boys and girls. Feeling ill at ease in the Berkshire environment, Hawthorne ultimately left, but William named the estate Tanglewood in his honor.

William and Caroline and their family went abroad for six years between 1855 and the early 1860s, first living in Paris and then Italy. On their return just before the Civil War broke out, William occupied the small red cottage year around. When Caroline built the big house at Tanglewood a few years later, he remained in the small red farmhouse, enjoying his reclusive life for the next thirty years. She kept hoping that he would join her and leave that drafty farmhouse. But he stayed there. In 1890, the place burned to the ground. Today, a replica of the house, built in 1947 by the National Federation of Music Clubs, marks the spot.

Tanglewood and The Boston Symphony Orchestra

In August 1934, members of the New York Philharmonic, directed by Henry Hadley, gave three outdoor concerts at Interlaken. The music-loving residents who had initiated this venture were so pleased that they incorporated the Berkshire Symphonic Festival and repeated the event during the next summer. The following year, they invited Serge Koussevitzky and the Boston Symphony Orchestra to participate. On August 13, 1936, the Boston Symphony Orchestra gave three concerts under a large tent at Holmwood, a former Vanderbilt estate, later the Center at Foxhollow—almost 15,000 people attended.

In the winter of 1936, Mrs. Gorham Brooks and Miss Mary Aspinwall Tappan, a descendant of William and Caroline, gave Tanglewood, the Tappan family estate, with its buildings and 210 acres of lawns and meadows to the Boston Symphony Orchestra and its conductor Serge Koussevitzky. On August 5, 1937, the festival's largest crowd so far assembled under a tent for the first Tanglewood concert, an all-Beethoven program.

"From the nearby Berkshire Hunt and Country Club, where he and his wife had been put up in the best suite, Conductor Serge Koussevitzky of the Boston Symphony drove over to Tanglewood, noted with approval that a tan tent, 280 feet by 120 feet and 60 feet high at its peak, had been raised on the property. Dr. Koussevitzky entered the tent, commanded that two sticks be clicked together before the big plywood orchestra shell. Listening judiciously from the rear of the tent, Conductor Koussevitzky heard the distinct click, beamed, and pronounced: "Fine! Fine! Very good!" The next evening, as the sun dropped behind the green hills, Conductor Koussevitzky stood on the podium in un-summery white tie and tail coat, tapped his baton, raised his arms for the portentous opening of Beethoven's Leonore Overture No. 3." *(Time Magazine, 1937)*

The second weekend the orchestra presented an all-Wagner concert, which was marred by rain and thunder. During intermission, one of the festival's founders had made an appeal to raise funds for the building of a permanent structure. By 1940, the Berkshire Music Center (now the Tanglewood Music Center) began its operations.

Today, Tanglewood is the summer home of the Boston Symphony Orchestra. Thousands of music lovers converge on it during June, July, and August to enjoy not only the music, but also the extraordinary views of the rolling countryside.

The Ghost at Tanglewood

In 1987, The Boston Symphony Orchestra acquired the Highwood estate, significantly expanding their property. The three-story Victorian home, known as Highwood Manor, provides rehearsal and office space.

It wasn't until the 1990s that musicians and staff realized that a ghost was in residence. In 1992, according to various reporters, staff members began noticing the presence of a classical music-loving ghost. Unseen hands smoothed a staff member's hair; doors opened and closed; and water faucets turned on and off — all by themselves! Conductor John Williams, who wrote the music for many great films including *Star Wars* and *E.T.*, joined other orchestra members in a search for the ghost.

The ghost frightened even composer and Conductor Leonard Bernstein. Bernstein was sitting at a bay window of the house two months before he died in October 1990. "He flew out of that window seat," recalled one staff member who was with him at the time. "He threw his arms toward the sky, saying, 'what is it that's here? Who is it?'"

Other workers have searched for the ghost and even offered to sleep overnight. Some have reported close encounters. One staff member leaves the house when she is alone because she is "spooked." A festival spokeswoman said she heard someone sigh behind her when she dropped by the house at night during a performance intermission. No one was there, of course, other than her own trembling self.

Tanglewood workers say the ghostly happenings seem to multiply during the summer after they placed a series of photographs of Tanglewood greats, including Bernstein, on the walls of hallways on the second floor.

Some say that the ghost was the spirit of 37-year-old Oreb Andrews, who died in 1822 when a tree fell on him and was awakened in 1986—when workmen disturbed a memorial marker. But perhaps the ghost is Caroline, who, with the expansion of Tanglewood, is hoping that her husband would come join her to enjoy the music and the flowers. Perhaps she sees that familiar hall and the light from his study; maybe she can smell his pipe; and perhaps if she made enough noise, she might just get his attention.

DIRECTIONS: From Mass Pike (I-90), Exit 2, take US-20 west (right at Mass Pike off-ramp) for approximately four miles (through Lee). Turn left onto MA-183 south. After 0.25 miles, MA-183 south merges with MA-7A north. After 0.2 miles, MA-7A forks to the right, stay straight on MA-183 south for another mile. The main entrance to Tanglewood will be on the left.

The Old Coot

The beautiful Berkshire Hills have supposedly been haunted for centuries. Many tales are told of spirits in the forest, apparitions, mythical animals, and of those who have wandered into the forest, never to return again. The Old Coot is one of the more famous.

When the War between the States began in 1861, everyone was caught up in the war fever that swept the land that spring and summer. All over western Massachusetts, companies of militia were forming. Only three days after the surrender of Fort Sumter on April 18, large public rallies were held where more men enlisted. By April 24, women in many towns and villages had vowed to sew the uniforms of the local company. As the cloth arrived, some women even sewed publicly in the town halls. Poets recited verses; flags waved; and brass bands played. Those Yankee farmers, trades people, and artisans had become local heroes who would "whip the secesh" in a short time, or so they believed.

Men kissed wives; sons kissed their mothers and the girls wore their prettiest dresses and clung to their handkerchiefs. Those who stayed at home urged their men to defend the union to the death. And, of course, there was much talk of honor.

About fifty percent of all Northerners still lived on farms when the war began. Most farmers were not rich, but they were able to feed their own family and produce enough food to sell in the cities.

One of the men who joined the Union force was a North Adams farmer named William Saunders. He kissed his wife Belle goodbye, saying, "I have to go." He left home to be part of what he thought would be an exhilarating and ennobling experience. Hugging him hard, she said, "Mr. Sanders, my heart will beat anxiously for you and your well being, but I will tend to the home fires and care for our two children." He patted her shoulder. He knew she was proud of her man.

That first year was a hard one for Belle. She wasn't just knitting by the fireside and keeping the home fires burning; she and her children depended on her labor for their food, fuel, clothing and home. She had to plow, cultivate, seed, weed, water, and harvest.

About a year later, Belle received a telegraph that William had been seriously wounded and was in a military hospital. That would be the last time she would hear of him.

Life was becoming harder for both Northerners and Southerners on the home front. The military needed everything that anyone could make, so businesses that produced and sold food and other goods raised their prices. Belle, like many others, had to struggle to make ends meet. Each morning, she shouldered her hoe and walked to the field. At one point, life had held such promise, and now there was nothing. If she knew William was dead, she could accept it — or at least she thought she could. But he was missing, and that ambiguity overwhelmed her. It was hard to know when to give up hope and to begin grieving.

Pumpkins in the field

She felt weary, depressed, and totally worn down, trying to maintain the farm and provide food for her family. She wept endlessly. She wept when she fed the chickens, when she cooked for her children, and when she went to bed. She never heard herself crying. Her grief was a part of her, heard only in her bones like the sound of the winter wind moaning around the house. All she had was her children and a big demanding farm.

In need of help, she offered Isaac, a local man, room and board if he would work the farm with her. As the months passed, she began to be aware again of the birds chirping, the bees droning, and the butterflies darting among the flowers. In between all that harrowing, tilling, seeding and harvesting, she saw a chance to shed her bitter unhappy self. She could begin life over again. Looking at Isaac, she felt something strong and solid that a woman could warm her hands and heart upon. So she married Isaac, who became a father to her children.

As the years passed, as each crop and beast followed its appointed time with the cows having their calves, the ewes dropping their kids, the corn being harvested, she felt thankful for her family and the presence of love in her life. A rounded and graceful fullness replaced her thinness. Smiles lit her face. A new baby filled the cradle.

In 1865, several months after the war had ended, a bearded, ragged man, wearing a tattered Union uniform, stepped off the train at the North Adams station. His hair hung long; his face was haggard. William was home, but no one came to say "Hurrah, Hurrah" because he was long forgotten. Whistling as he walked to his farm, he contemplated the reunion that would take place. His wife would hold him in her warm firm arms. He would stroke her long brown hair. They would slaughter a chicken and eat like he hadn't for years. His stomach rumbled in anticipation. Probably his children wouldn't recognize him — he had been gone so long. He wondered how tall his boy was now.

When he arrived at the farm, he saw his wife bend her head toward the man besides her; he heard his children calling another man "daddy."

Crushed, he turned on his heels and walked away. It occurred to him that his life was valueless now—no one cared. He was consigned to homelessness. He headed toward Mt. Greylock, where he built a shack in the remote Bellows Pipe. He lived the rest of his days in his forest home. Occasionally, he would take a job as a hired hand, known to locals only as the "Old Coot." The war and passage of time had destroyed his appearance, and no one recognized him.

The locals say that he even worked on his own farm on occasion. Maybe he even sat down to meals with his family, but they never knew him. People say the Old Coot was insane, but whether it was war-related stress or grief at losing his family, no one knows.

One winter's day, hunters came upon the shack to find the Old Coot lying on the ground. But as they checked to see if he was dead, they saw a strange man-shaped shadow dart out of the shack, heading up to the cool evergreens near the top of the mountain.

Ever since, hunters and hikers have reported seeing a shadowy, bedraggled form walking through the woods of Mount Greylock. There across the swaying treetops, this spectral figure looks over the valleys and mountains into three adjoining states. He has the world at his feet, but he is all alone for eternity.

When Johnny comes marching home again,
Hurrah! Hurrah!
We'll give him a hearty welcome then
Hurrah! Hurrah!
The men will cheer and the boys will shout
The ladies they will all turn out
And we'll all feel gay,
When Johnny comes marching home.
Patrick Sarsfield Gilmore

Tale of Two Sisters

Overlooking the town of Lenox is an 1820 English Tudor country inn surrounded by acres of gardens and woodland. From its windows you can see the natural beauty and mystery of the Berkshire landscape. In its grand library, you can relax in Queen Anne chairs in front of the black marble fireplace or perhaps you would rather play the 1898 Steinway opera grand that dominates the music room.

This lovely inn is one of the haunted houses of the Berkshires. The neighborhood children tell stories about the tree-shrouded Tudor style house and its ghosts. The current owners of Whistler's Inn, Richard Chase Mears and Joan Mears, say the inn has been a haven of supernatural happenings, from water oozing from unusual places to strange electrical surges. They report strange sensations when visiting the attic: they feel odd shifts in the air; chilled breaths that raise the hairs on the back of the neck. Members of the Mears family and guests of the inn have reported seeing apparitions, mostly women.

Before becoming an inn, it was the home of Ross Whistler, nephew of the painter, James Abbott McNeil Whistler. The latter was well known for his art, particularly Arrangement in Grey and Black, No. 1: Portrait of the Artist's Mother, that was later acquired by the French government. Ross' claim to fame was that he was a railroad baron.

When he died suddenly in 1927, his grieving widow hired Nancy Hedwall, a young Swedish émigré, to be a live-in companion and servant. Suddenly, Nancy had a blue gingham frock with a large wraparound apron to wear in the mornings. In the afternoon, she changed to her black afternoon dress with a tiny frilled apron and placed a starched white cap on her blond curls.

She greeted Mrs. Whistler's callers and served tea in the grey painted sitting room with the emerald green ceiling.

Nancy had her own domain, which was part sitting room and part workroom. Close to it was the storage room, the linen closet with its large oak drawers and brass fittings, and the china cupboards. The large bunch of keys she carried at her waist signaled her responsibility. Everything from spice boxes to jewelry boxes had to be kept locked.

Besides anticipating Mrs. Whistler's every wish, answering the door and the telephone, waiting on guests, running errands, and endlessly washing, ironing, and sponging, she had to be sure the fireplaces were stocked with coal, the grates were clean, and that meals were served at least three times a day — not counting tea time.

Of course, she was pleased to have a job that gave her room and board, and even uniforms, but she didn't like working this hard. Young and pretty, she wanted time to play, to dream of a life of freedom, to contemplate being in love. She couldn't do that if she were going to be responsible for managing the large house. So Nancy began to demand more help.

Mrs. Whistler brought her a new iron. "Look," she said, "ironing no longer requires long hours in the kitchen handling a hot, heavy iron." But Nancy still complained.

So Mrs. Whistler brought her one of the new electric vacuums. "You won't have to remove the rugs and curtains every spring and fall to beat the dirt out of them. Now, you have your own vacuum."

But Nancy didn't want a vacuum. She wanted someone to do some of her work, preferably the cooking. She hated to cook.

When Mrs. Whistler didn't pay any attention to her complaints, Nancy began scorching the morning toast and giving her runny soft-boiled eggs on her morning breakfast tray. She cooked the Sunday roast until it was gray, the Brussels sprouts until they were soggy, and the potatoes not at all. When guests arrived for dinner, she served a stringy chicken, mushy cauliflower, great hunks of carrots, and a tough chocolate soufflé. To avoid any suspicion that she was deliberately sabotaging dinners, she also forgot to iron the newspaper and didn't brush Mrs. Whistler's riding habit.

After three weeks of Nancy's campaign, Mrs. Whistler gave a deep sigh and succumbed. She knew her comfort depended on a happy housekeeper, but where would she get more help? Anticipating this question, Nancy volunteered that her older sister, Helma, could act as a cook, and Helma's husband, Paul Anthony, could become the chauffeur. That way, Nancy could have familiar faces around who could speak her native tongue, and Mrs. Whistler would have a chauffeur and a cook who could make a nourishing soup or an acceptable omelet for lunch and provide richly buttered scones, watercress and cucumber sandwiches, and other suitable components of a lavish afternoon tea.

Helma wanted to leave her homeland. "We could have a much better life, Paul, in the United States than here in Sweden."

"We can make a fortune in America. And now Nancy has found us jobs."

Ah, life was good, they agreed as they packed their belongings and came to the United States.

From New York City, they traveled to Lenox, Massachusetts. Nancy jingled her keys happily as she showed them the house where they would work. The walnut paneled library was furnished with Chinese porcelain and Chippendale chairs balanced by comfortable sofas upholstered in dark green velvet. The Oriental carpet was a swirl of blues, golds, and greens. The music room had Louis XVI palace furniture and mirrors, French candelabras and putti, Persian rugs, and a white marble fireplace. Over the mantel hung an oil portrait of a lady spinning wool. Across from it was a massive portrait of Mary Magdalene, looking repentant.

Helma's eyes popped when she saw her new kitchen. "It's one of those electric ranges. Oh my, look at those brass switches. Nancy, luckily we still have the old wood-fired stove. That's good. What's that funny thing?"

"An electric refrigerator. No more ice box."

Helma's eyes rolled. Life in America was good. The kitchen still had the huge dresser with cupboards below and its shelves laden with a full dinner service of 126 pieces, all of which needed to be washed once a week. A kitchen table stood in the center of the room. It had to be scrubbed and scoured white with soap and soda every day along with the stone flag floor.

Nancy danced around the kitchen, pointing out the dumb-waiter, the knife sharpener, and the long row of bells with room indicators above. There were knives of all kinds—from mighty carving knives to small mincing knives, and two kinds of grat-ers; one for nutmegs and one for breadcrumbs. There were aluminum spoons, a flour sifter, a mortar and pestle and an egg whisk. Helma's eyes sparkled.

To one side of the door was the larder, with small unglazed windows covered in fine mesh. Ceiling hooks held several hams. The adjacent scullery had three oak-framed sinks and three plate racks. Above the sink were shelves with gleaming copper pans and white storage jugs.

"It will be a day's walk to get around here," said Helma hap-pily.

Featured on the Travel Channel, this 1820 English Tudor Manor has a romantic history attached to it.

"You will be the queen of the kitchen," Nancy said, "and I'll be the queen of the house."

Helma smiled. As a cook, she wore white ribbed cotton with a white apron and an additional white cloth pinned over her large bosom. Nancy might have her key ring, but Helma had her kitchen with its copper pots and pans.

Paul was similarly pleased when he saw the large square garage with the large black Dodge. He would have his own domain. There, he could feel his omnipotence, which he might not in the house with three women to contend with.

Nancy and Helma were like many sisters. Helma knew that Nancy loved to lie on the grass and braid daisy chains. She knew that Nancy liked stories of unrequited love, undying love, mistaken identity, ambitious courtiers, and marriages of convenience. She had watched Nancy's eyes sparkle when she heard descriptions of the upper classes and their activities such as theatre events, fittings, suppers, assemblies, and balls. She also knew that back in Sweden Nancy had been accused of flirting with their married neighbor, which led to her being sent to the United States. She scolded herself for remembering a bad time. She should thank her lucky stars that Nancy could get Paul and her to the United States of America.

Helma floured her table and her rolling pin and began to flatten her piecrust. She was the practical older sister. She was the one who saved the money, while Nancy was the one who spent it. She was Aesop's ant who industriously transported large crumbs of bread from site to storage while Nancy's grasshopper reclined on a blade of grass, enjoying the sun. Nancy dreamed of passionate love, while Helma saw sex as something that she might do in the darkened bedroom as quietly as possible. She could smell the ham cooking in the oven. She flipped the piecrust over and rolled it thinner. It was good that they could work together in this large lovely home for only one person.

One spring afternoon when Helma was peeling potatoes for dinner, Nancy followed Paul to the garage. She leaned across the Dodge he was polishing and asked, "So how do you like it here?"

"I like it fine."

"Maybe we should go for a walk. We could find some berries for Helma." She eyed him in the most suggestive way. He thought she had bedroom eyes. He was sure that he could have her then and there, but he paid attention to the small voice in his head that warned him to be cautious. The last thing he needed to be doing as a new immigrant was bedding his wife's sister. And so he sent her back to the house.

Later, he found himself wondering about her. He wanted to see her again, to explore the possibilities. Then he was ashamed. Why would he ever cheat on Helma?

"Why not?" asked that small imp. Helma was always tired and going to bed early. She was always worrying about money and looking for opportunities to get ahead. He had been happy enough in Sweden; at least he was in a city with some excitement. Here, he was back in the country again.

The next day, around the time Helma started preparing dinner, Paul found he was waiting for Nancy. He experienced a rush of excitement. He couldn't wait for her to arrive. He wanted to study her again.

When she entered the garage, he was waiting for her. "I brought you a coffee," she said.

He took the coffee, sipped from it, and sat down in the driver's seat of the car. She smiled and got into the passenger's seat.

"Nice coffee," he murmured.

"Nice as me?" Nancy licked her lower lip.

He put his arm on the back of her seat. Immediately, she took hold of his hand and licked his palm while gazing up at him.

He was intrigued.

She leaned forward and kissed him on the mouth. He didn't resist.

When Paul came into the kitchen, Helma glanced at him. He wondered if he looked different. He stepped closer to her, and she caught his scent: automobile polish and soap. Five years, she thought, and he's hardly changed. The same youthful tilt of his head, the same laugh lines, the same blond hair. She felt the old pull drawing her towards him.

Once dinner was over and the dishes washed and dried, Helma looked quizzically at him. "You're very quiet, Paul. Is there a reason?"

"No. Come and sit with me." He patted the chair next to him. But then Nancy came in. She looked at Paul in an oddly significant way. His hand dropped.

Watching the interaction between the two made Helma uncertain. She turned away. "No, I'm tired. I'm going to bed."

Helma lay in bed, trying to relax. The swish of Nancy's starched housekeeper's black uniform always signaled when she was coming into the room. It looked quite good with her blonde hair. She, on the other hand, wore a cook's apron, and her hair always smelled of dinner. Even the smell of a succulent rib roast can dismay the most loving of husbands.

The next three days Nancy didn't go to the garage. Paul found that he had lost his concentration and also his polishing rag.

Then she reappeared. When he stepped out of the garage shadows, she moved toward him, put her arms around, and kissed him on the mouth. He was instantly aroused. He pulled her into the back seat of the Dodge. Her embrace was so hot that he could swear he smelled smoke and heard a distant rumble. He kissed her eyes, her nose, and her lips with furious joy.

During the next several months, Nancy would go to Paul while Helma was peeling, mashing, chopping, and cutting. Sometimes she would meet him in the attic, where they would make love in between the old suitcases and trunks. Mrs. Whistler's old dress form and a hat stand decorated with out-of-fashion hats were the bemused spectators. But usually she and Paul would lie in the back seat of the big black Dodge. She was certain that she would have her "happily ever after," if he would just say that he loved her, but he didn't.

In the kitchen, Helma kneaded, grated, whipped, and stirred. She would sit at the kitchen table, beating eggs and melted butter into a warm bowl of potatoes that she had just boiled and mashed. A pot of yellow split-pea soup seasoned with pork was simmering on the stove, and its fragrance overwhelmed the kitchen. The smell of the soup and the warmth of the kitchen created a secure and comfortable atmosphere, but she knew that was a sham. She also knew that if she confronted what lay beneath that feeling of security and warmth that her life would change. And so Helma took her time adding flour to the bowl of mashed potatoes and tenderly mixing it in with her hands. The rhythmic kneading of the warm potato dough soothed her. Her cooking was an act of reverence in honor of the people who would enjoy it later.

Then one evening when she was supposed to be stuffing the turkey, she no longer could resist the temptation of knowing what was happening. Helma burst into the garage. Looking at the bouncing car with the two bodies in back, Helma cried out, but her words were unintelligible. She burst into tears. Bringing her hands to her face, she sobbed as if her heart was breaking.

The sisters still weren't talking when Paul took the car out one rainy evening. Surging forward, enjoying the speed, Paul wasn't aware of the truck coming towards him. The truck rammed the Dodge, pushing it backward with such great speed that it went into a tailspin. Paul clutched at the wheel, pressed his foot down hard on the brake, as his car went into a terrifying skid. The Dodge slid across the road, spun around, slid backward and went off the road, rolling over and over as it fell into a deep valley. The sisters buried him in the cemetery across the street from the Whistler residence.

When Paul died, some of Nancy did too. All she could think was he would never tell her that he loved her. She would have to live without him for the rest of her life. Even worse she would have to live without him while she maintained house for another woman who had lost her man and live with her sister whose man she took. This would be the seventh circle of hell for her.

Meanwhile, Helma had to look at the woman every day who had taken her husband's love from her. Dinner still lingered in her hair; she still wore a cook's uniform, but she no longer had her husband creeping guiltily into her bed still smelling of another woman. Listening to the creaks of the house and the gusts rattling the window, she imagined spending a lifetime under this roof: the years of silence, the unchanging rituals. There would be some comfort in knowing at each dawn how the day would go: no surprises, no turmoil, no arguments, and no suspicions. Rising from bed, reaching for the same clothing, and doing the same thing. Within the walls, the rituals would continue unchanging.

Eventually, Helma died, dried up and bitter. Then Nancy died from her guilt. Mrs. Whistler buried them, although they still were barely speaking, next to Paul.

Today, there are certain cold spots and warm spots in the inn. In the still air you can sense a presence. Is it the illicit lovers meeting to renew their passion? Is it Helma, the eternally betrayed? Is it the three servants, together, who cannot rest in peace?

DIRECTIONS: Take the Mass Pike to Exit 2, Lee. Follow Route 20 north through Lee. Route 20 merges with Route 7. Continue north to Route 7A Lenox, which will take you through the village of Lenox. As you pass through the village, you will climb a hill and to your left you will see a large white church at the top of the hill, on the corner of 7A and Greenwood Avenue. Whistler's Inn is also located on the corner directly across Greenwood Avenue and from the church.

The Bloody Pit

The Berkshire countryside is beautiful with pastures stretching to its very edges. There's the occasional cow and many wild flowers swaying in the soft breezes. The birds sing, and Beethoven's Pastoral plays somewhere in your mind. Slowly descending a gentle slope, you arrive at the depths of these purple shrouded hills. The wooded sides begin pressing against you. The sun, which has been a steady beam, is reduced to pale shafts seeking the ground. Rock walls covered with lichens tumble along the sides. The air begins to smell wet and moldy, like a badly cleaned toilet. Suddenly, the dark hole of the Hoosic Tunnel, with its ancient dank smell, looms at you.

The opening is only twenty feet in diameter in a mountain that towers above it at seventeen hundred feet *(The Atlantic Monthly, p. 303)*. Listed on the Historic American Engineering Survey and the National Register, the 4.75 mile long Hoosic Tunnel is a railroad tunnel through the Hoosic Range, an extension of Vermont's Green Mountains. An engineering marvel, its east portal is in Florida, Massachusetts; the west, in North Adams, Massachusetts. Begun in 1851 and completed in 1875, it was the second longest tunnel in the world and the longest tunnel in North America until the Moffat Tunnel west of Denver was built in the 1920s. East of the Rocky Mountains, it is the longest transportation tunnel.

This illustrious history is accompanied by fearful whispers. Many think the ghosts of the almost two hundred men who died constructing the Hoosic Tunnel still lurk within its dark, clammy interior. People have reported seeing lanterns sway and hearing the sounds of chisels and the wails of the dying men. Some scoff at the ghost stories, but no one likes to be there for long.

Tunnel Construction

The city of North Adams, in the northwest corner of Massachusetts, has abundant waterpower, which led to a booming textile and shoe industry in the nineteenth century. The Berkshire Mountains, however, were a sturdy barrier to commerce. Those rugged hills, which are intersected by valleys and streams of water, separated the Berkshires from the rest of the world. In 1819, legislators proposed a canal to transport goods and raw materials between Boston and points west, but the enormity of the project overwhelmed its supporters. Irish, Italian, and French Canadian workers migrated to the city in search of work in its factories and mills, and the industrial base of the town grew substantially between 1830 and 1845.

With the advent of the steam locomotive, the tunnel project was reevaluated. In 1848, with the slogan "On to Hoosic, on to the West," the Troy and Greenfield line was established, and the tunnel project was a reality. On May 20, 1853, the *New York Daily Times* reported:

> The Hoosic Tunnel, on the scale adopted by the Railroad Company, is a work of stupendous grandeur to contemplate. Its accomplishment will certainly be a proud day for American Railway enterprise. It will be 8,000 yards or nearly five miles in continuous length and in cost and masonry will be scarcely second to the great Leeds and Manchester Tunnel in England.

With the bore initially planned to cost $2 million, work began in 1851. Hundreds of miners, using mostly black powder, shovels, picks, and their hands began to bore through Hoosic Mountain. During the summer of 1852, Wilson's Patented Stone-Cutting Machine® began boring into the east side of the mountain. After excavating about ten feet, the machine died.

Using just manpower, hand-drills, and gunpowder meant slow progress at both portals. The tunnel's construction project required the excavation of two million tons (1,800,000 metric tons) of rock. Tunnel builders resorted to hand digging and hand drills and later used the Burleigh Rock Drill®, one of the first pneumatic drills. The project also saw the first large-scale commercial use of electric blasting caps and nitroglycerin, an effective but extremely unstable explosive.

By the late nineteenth century, North Adams was the commercial and industrial center of North Berkshire. The construction of the Hoosic Tunnel (1851-1875) provided more direct rail service to urban centers and to their markets. Originally estimated to cost $2 million, the final cost of the tunnel was more than $14 million. The last passenger train traversed the tunnel in 1958, but the tunnel is still an important link in the freight route from New England to the Midwest.

The Murders

During the almost twenty-five years of construction, more than two hundred men had died in what was called the "Bloody Pit." They died in fires, explosions, tunnel collapses, and in one case, by the hand of another. The events that occurred in 1865 give the tunnel its enduring reputation for ghosts.

In 1865, nitroglycerin was introduced to America and the Hoosic Tunnel construction crew had the honor of being among the first crews to use it. On the afternoon of March 20, 1865, three explosive experts named Ned Brinkman, Billy Nash and Ringo Kelley decided to use nitro to continue their work on the tunnel. They placed a charge and then ran back toward a safety bunker. Brinkman and Nash never made it. For some unknown reason, Ringo Kelley set off the charge prematurely. Tons of rock buried his two co-workers. He walked away unhurt.

The East Portal of the Hoosic tunnel

Soon after their deaths, Kelley vanished, leading to suspicion that the deaths of Brinkman and Nash may not have been an accident after all. He was not seen again until March 30, 1866 (note: this is almost one year later), when his body was discovered two miles inside the tunnel—at almost the exact spot where Brinkman and Nash had been killed. Deputy Sheriff Charles F. Gibson estimated that he had been strangled between midnight and 3:30 a.m. that morning. Although Kelley's death was thoroughly investigated, no suspects were ever identified and the crime went unsolved.

Of course, the construction workers had their own suspicions about who murdered Ringo Kelley. They believed that Brinkman and Nash had returned from the dead to kill Kelley. Certain that the tunnel was cursed, many of them refused to enter it again. Some of them even left the job permanently as the workers began avoiding the dark and brooding place, with the deep shadows and dripping water. That slowed the construction of the tunnel down even more.

The Deaths

A means of ventilating the coal exhaust from the tunnel, the central shaft was used to hoist rock and ferry workmen in large copper buckets. The workers rode to their work site, sometimes sitting on the swaying bucket, sometimes standing on its rim. This method of transportation was so fast that the 1,030-foot descent took only two minutes.

In the March 1882 *Atlantic Monthly*, N. H. Eggleston described it:

"At every descent of the bucket it seemed as though those in it were being dashed down the dark pit to almost certain destruction. Speed was necessary, and the machinery was arranged so that the descent of over a thousand feet was made in a little more than a minute. The sensations experienced by those who descended the shaft were peculiar. First, there was the sensation of rapid, helpless falling through space in the darkness; then, as the speed was at last abruptly arrested, it seemed for a moment as though the motion had been reversed, and one were being as rapidly elevated to the surface again."

The Central Shaft was the scene of some the worst accidents in building the tunnel. The shaft was dangerous: one time, a sharpened drill rolled into the pit, impaling a workman; another time, a worker fell down the chimney.

On October 17, 1867, an ill-designed lamp called a "Gasometer" leaked naphtha fumes into the hoist house. It exploded, sending the building up in flames. Thirteen men were working in the shaft, which was more than five hundred feet deep, at the time. First, more than three hundred newly sharpened drill bits fell on them. Then the hoist mechanism and burning sections of the structure fell, and the shaft began to fill with water.

> *A terrible accident occurred at the Hoosic Tunnel, on Saturday, by which thirteen men were either killed outright or suffocated to death. The Gasoline Works at the mouth of the shaft exploded and burned, falling down the shaft and burying the whole gang of workmen at the bottom. The bodies will not be extricated for some days.*
>
> *The New York Times, October 21, 1867*

A fifty-year-old workman named Mallory had volunteered to be lowered into the shaft. At 4 a.m., he was lowered in a bucket, but returned to the surface a few minutes later, nearly unconscious from the fumes. On recovery, he said he could see nothing but water and burnt timbers. There was no hope for survivors.

Within a few days the 538-foot shaft had filled with water, which, with the fallen timbers, made it impossible to recover the bodies of the dead men. Some bodies began to surface, but it wasn't until a year later that all the bodies were recovered and identified.

Glenn Drohan, a *North Adams Transcript* correspondent, reported: "During the time the miners were missing, villagers told strange tales of vague shapes and muffled wails near the water-filled pit. Workmen claimed to see the lost miners carrying picks and shovels through a shroud of mist and snow on the mountaintop. The ghostly apparitions would appear briefly, then vanish, leaving no footprints in the snow, giving no answer to the miner's calls."

As soon as the last of the bodies were found and given a decent burial though, Drohan stated, the bizarre visitations ceased. These dead men had apparently found rest, but some of the victims of the "Bloody Pit" had not. Even after the apparitions stopped appearing, the eerie moanings in the tunnel continued and the men remained terrified.

The tunnel was never clear of the smoke and gas resulting from the trains. A fan was installed at the central shaft, but it was ineffective. The darkness, the coal gas, and almost ninety daily trains led to many rear-end collisions. One such collision in 1892 left four men dead (Byron, p. 50), another one the following year killed one person. And, tunnel workmen were either killed or crippled by trains that they couldn't see or hear approaching.

A cloud of smoke pervades it through its whole length, wafting backward and forward, to some extent by the occasional winds.... so that practically no one can see more than a few yards, or rods, at the most within the great cavern. No artificial light, not even the headlights of the locomotives, can penetrate the darkness for any considerable distance. The engineer sees nothing but feels his way, by faith and simple push of steam, through the five miles of solemn gloom.

(The Atlantic Monthly p. 305)

The Hauntings

In 1868, Mr. Dunn, who worked with the construction company, contacted Paul Travers, a mechanical engineer and a respected Civil War cavalry officer, requesting that he examine the tunnel. Apparently, the workers complained constantly of hearing a man's voice cry out in agony. Consequently, they refused to enter the half-completed tunnel after sundown. Dunn was certain that the winds sweeping off the mountainside made the wailing sounds, but work had slowed down so drastically that he requested an outside investigator.

On September 8, 1868, Travers and Dunn visited the site. The well-respected former military officer later wrote a letter to his sister, telling her about his experience: "Dunn and I entered the tunnel at exactly 9 p.m. We traveled about two miles into the shaft and then we stopped to listen. As we stood there in the cold silence, we both heard what truly sounded like a man groaning in pain ... Yet, when we turned up the wicks on our lamps, there were no other human beings in the shaft except ... us. I wonder?" (Byron, p. 67)

Based on the account of a Dr. Clifford J. Owen, the haunting also began to take on other characteristics as well. James R. McKinstrey, a drilling operations superintendent, took Owen to the tunnel on June 25, 1872. It is thought that they were looking for the ghosts who haunted the shaft.

The two men traveled about two miles into the tunnel and then halted to rest. Only their dim lamps lit the shaft. Owen later described the tunnel as being "as cold and as dark as a tomb." The two of them stood there talking for a few minutes, and then they heard a strange, mournful sound. Owen said it sounded like someone in great pain. He wrote:

The next thing I saw was a dim light coming along the tunnel in a westerly direction. At first, I believed that it was probably a workman with a lantern. Yet, as the light grew closer, it took on a strange blue color and appeared to change in shape into the form of a human being with no head. The light seem to be floating along about a foot or two above the tunnel floor ... The headless form came so close that I could have reached out and touched it, but I was too terrified to move.

The light remained motionless, as though watching them, then it hovered off toward the east end of the tunnel and vanished. Owen and McKinstrey were understandably stunned. (Byron, p. 68)

Owens later wrote that while he was "above all a realist" and that he was not "prone to repeating gossip and wild tales that defy a reasonable explanation," he was unable to "deny what James McKinstrey and I witnessed with our own eyes."

Strangeness continued at the Hoosic Tunnel when it opened. On October 16, 1874, a local hunter named Frank Webster vanished near Hoosic Mountain. Three days later, a search party found him, stumbling along the banks of the Deerfield River, in a state of shock, mumbling incoherently and falling down. He told his rescuers that strange voices had ordered him into the Hoosic Tunnel. When he was inside, he saw ghostly figures wandering around and that invisible hands had snatched his hunting rifle away from him. They then used it to beat him. He couldn't remember leaving the tunnel. Members of the search party recalled that Webster did not have his rifle when he was found and the cuts and abrasions on his head and body seemed to bear evidence of a beating.

Later that same year, when the tunnel headings were completed, workmen removed rocks from the tunnel and began grading the line and laying track. On February 9, 1875, the first train went through the tunnel, pulling three flatcars and a boxcar. A group of 125 people had come along for the ride. According to the news stories about the event, North Adams had just become the "Western Gateway" to the rest of New England. But this was not enough to stop the strange stories from being told.

Some interesting specks and orbs of light that appear to be floating in the tunnel. Are these souls of the dearly departed still haunting the site of their gristly and untimely demise? Or just . . . specks? *Courtesy of Paul Oleskiewicz*

In the fall of 1875, Harlan Mulvaney, a fire tender on the Boston & Maine rail line, drove a wagonload of wood into the tunnel. He had gone just a short distance into the shaft when he suddenly turned his team around, whipped the horses and drove them madly out of the tunnel. A few days later, workers found the team and the wagon in the forest about three miles away from the tunnel. Harlan Mulvaney had disappeared forever.

The stories continued. One former railroad employee, Joseph Impoco, worked the Boston and Maine line for years. He firmly believed that the tunnel was haunted, but he was not afraid of the place. In fact, he credited the resident ghosts with saving his life on two separate occasions. On one afternoon, he was chipping away ice from the tracks when he heard a distinct voice telling him to "run, Joe, run!" He glanced back and saw a train bearing down on him! "Sure enough, there was No. 60 coming at me. Boy, did I jump back fast!" When he looked around to thank whoever had called out his name, no one was there. Later, he would recall that he had distinctly heard the voice before the train appeared. He also added that he had seen a man pass by, waving and swinging a torch, but he hadn't paid attention to anything but the shout. The voice, wherever it had come from, had saved his life.

Six weeks after the incident, Impoco was again working on the tracks. This time, he was using a heavy iron crow bar to free some freight cars that had become frozen on the tracks. He was prying at one of the steel wheels when he heard the loud, familiar voice again call out to him. "Joe! Joe! Drop it, Joe!" the voice called frantically. Impoco immediately released the bar and, instantly, more than 11,000 volts of electricity jolted it and threw it against the tunnel wall! The charge came from a short-circuited overhead power line. The unseen friend had saved Joe's life again.

A short time later, Impoco left his job and began working out of the area. Every year though, he would return to the Hoosic

Tunnel and pay a sort of "homage" to the ghost who saved his life. He was certain that if he failed to do this just one year, some tragedy would befall him. In 1977, Impoco's wife was ill and, rather than go to visit the tunnel, he stayed home with her. In October of that year, she died. Joe believed that her death was connected to his failure to journey to the Hoosic Tunnel.

Since the 1970s, ghost hunters and paranormal groups have investigated the tunnel. They also report hearing voices, seeing ghostly apparitions, and photographing globes of light or orbs that appear to be floating in the tunnel. Locals in the area still claim that strange winds, ghostly apparitions and eerie voices are experienced around and in the daunting tunnel. Clouds of smoke pervade it.

"The passing traveler sees only the archway at either end and masses of shapeless rock, which has been excavated and used in part as an embankment for railway approaches" *(The Atlantic Monthly, p. 303)*. Visitors who wish to visit Hoosic Tunnel should be aware of the dangers. The Boston & Maine Railroad still runs about four freight trains through the tunnel each day: therefore, you don't want to be in the tunnel, looking for orbs and listening for voices. If you're interested in the historical aspects of the tunnel, though, you can visit a museum that is dedicated to the site in the Western Gateway Heritage State Park.

DIRECTIONS: To the East Portal: Head west on Route 2 (Mohawk Trail) to the center of the town of Florida. One half mile before the Eastern Summit, take a right on Church Road, a steep dirt road. At the bottom take a right onto Whitcome Hill Road. Take a left on River Road at the Deerfield River. About one half mile or more on the right is a railroad crossing. The East Portal is up the tracks on the left.

To the West Portal: Head west on Route 2 (Mohawk Trail) past the Western Summit. West Shaft Street is on the left about 1.5 miles past the hairpin turn. The West Portal is not observable from the road. You will need to park on the right just before where the road bends right and goes down into North Adams. The West Portal is 3/10ths of a mile due west through the woods. (Note: You will be arrested for trespassing.)

Central Shaft, Shaft Head & Fan Building: Travel west on Route 2 (Mohawk Trail) through the town of Florida. Central Shaft Road is on your left about two miles past Whitcomb Summit. The shaft-head fan building is about 1.5 miles on the left.

The Restless Monk

One of the grand Berkshire mansions was the large, turreted Shadowbrook, which overlooked Stockbridge Bowl. Built in 1893 by New York banker and entrepreneur Anson Stokes, it had one hundred rooms, making it the third largest private residence in the United States under one roof at that time.

In 1922, The New England Province of the Society of Jesus purchased the property from Andrew Carnegie for use as a Jesuit novitiate. Later a major fire destroyed the mansion, killing four Jesuits and injuring six other priests and brothers. It was at this time that people began to see a ghostly monk. The Jesuits rebuilt the building, but ultimately closed the novitiate. The Kripalu Center for Yoga and Health opened at Shadowbrook on December 1, 1983.

Today, waiters, clerks, and long-time residents in the area insist that the restless spirit of a monk haunts Shadowbrook. We don't know why that monk was restless, but here is one possible reason…

By the turn of the twentieth century, the cottage era in Lenox and Stockbridge had become quite splendid. Captains of industry and robber barons built substantial mansions as shrines to their success. They employed workers to carve the wood, to bend the copper, and to cast the iron for their mansions—a new and influential class with infinite wealth had emerged. Life was very good for some, thought Harry.

He glanced up when she entered the crowded hall. Ah, he thought. This must be Lawrence's new wife, Octavia. She was fine-boned with creamy white skin and long, red hair. She certainly looked a good deal younger than Lawrence, who was at least twenty years older than he was.

Harry nodded to his friend Paul, who was standing with several other friends arguing again about whether bicycling on the village sidewalks should be allowed. Having heard the discussion before, Harry turned and met plump, upholstered Mrs. Crandall, who smiled at him.

"Well, Harry Lowell, how are you?" Next to her stood Octavia.

"Good afternoon. Mrs. Crandall."

She said, "I have someone for you to meet."

Harry bowed over Octavia's hand. "Welcome to Stockbridge."

"Thank you," she replied. She looked innocent, but he was sure that her beauty hid a more sultry side.

"You're Lawrence's new wife, Octavia," he murmured. Arrogant, just, and stern, Lawrence was one of the notable figures of his day in the New York legal world. Also a widower, he had raised a few eyebrows when he married Octavia. Much younger than he, she was known to be a follower of Isadora Duncan.

"A believer in Women Suffrage too," sniped Harry's mother when he had seen her for tea the day before. "You know what that means."

It didn't seem to mean much because once they were married Lawrence ignored his new wife. Many of the worthy Berkshire matrons didn't like Octavia, but no one actually said why they felt that way. Harry suspected that they disliked her style, her assertiveness, and her seeming flair. At least one stiffly corseted matron sniffed when Octavia walked past, "She's like those new-fangled Gibson Girls. She probably drinks cocktails too!"

Perhaps she was, thought Harry. But her shirtwaist with long sleeves and sleek skirt certainly was a lot freer and more practical than the braided wire bustles and petticoats worn by many of the women he knew. Despite her slender figure, his first wife had worn a boned corset, forcing the bust forward and cinching her waist to the requisite eighteen inches. Harry was positive that the severe corset had crushed her internal organs and weakened her back muscles, leaving her more vulnerable to illness. She had died seven years previously, but Harry still blamed himself – he was her protector after all – for not making her shed that contraption. Wasn't he supposed to have and hold her for better for worse, for richer for poorer, in sickness and in health? His grief had engulfed him for several years.

Animated groups of people filled the massive pale yellow marble gallery.

"And have you enjoyed your stay here?" he asked.

"I am just another one of the summer people." Octavia looked down at her feet briefly.

"Hmm." He looked about at the people discussing the next party, tomorrow's archery meet, and their tennis game. Was this all that life offered, he wondered?

"Well, the summer people are the essential livelihood of the Berkshires, after all, they tell me." She laughed, and Harry noticed her large eyes were the color of blue pansies. She was even more seductive close up.

"But I don't expect to be coddled one bit. I'd rather be more independent, if you know what I mean."

Harry thought he might know. He was tired of people waiting on him. He was tired of the rituals of this world. The days filled with people talking and laughing about church service, the Village Improvement Society, or the next dinner party didn't meet his needs. The new game of golf was wonderful, but it wasn't enough. He was tired of doing the same old thing in the same old way. He wanted to feel intensely again. He owned an excellent pair of horses, but even they stood forlornly in the stable, hoping that sometime they would gallop through the Berkshire Hills again.

"You mean you walk to and from the post office when you are not playing at tennis or croquet?" he asked. So many of the women didn't.

"No. I am a cyclist."

"Ah. They say the Berkshires are a cyclist's paradise."

"Oh, but it is. The views are wonderful. And biking allows you to be so free." Her smile was broad.

"Is it true that the bicycle has done more to emancipate women than anything else in the world — like Susan B. Anthony said?"

"It certainly has helped us to be seen as stronger and less helpless." She laughed. "I like that."

"We have to make the roads better though."

"And by the time that happens maybe we will really be in a horseless age." Her eyes sparkled.

"Without horses, they say, our streets will be cleaner, accidents will be less frequent; and traffic jams less likely."

"I wonder," she said, "but certainly it will take less time to travel from one place to another." Those haunting eyes were lit with intelligence, and her shape was delightfully feminine.

"Do you play croquet?" Harry asked. "They have a game tomorrow."

"I do."

"Perhaps I will see you there."

"Perhaps."

Harry noted happily to himself that she was reciprocating his attention. On the other hand, she was a married woman — perhaps unhappily so, if he were to believe the gossip.

The next morning a breeze blew steadily from the hills. Canopies of white clouds threw cool shadows over the croquet court, where many people were playing. Harry found himself looking for Octavia and ignoring his friends. Half way through the course, Octavia knocked her ball into the woods, murmured her excuses, and disappeared after the ball. Harry went after her. He found her in a rocky glen, sitting on a large fallen tree. Her hair was in curly disorder around her slender neck. He sat down beside her.

"Thinking or dreaming?" he asked.

"The latter of course." She laughed. "Don't you ever wish you could start over?"

"You mean a new life with different choices?"

"Yes… I wish I could escape from here." Lifting her hands, she took the pins from her hat and laid it on the log.

"Oh?" Birds chirruped, bees hummed, butterflies darted – he suddenly felt the softness of the afternoon in his bones.

"I'm too young to live this settled kind of existence. It should be illegal to marry before you've had several serious beaus, felt strongly about at least three things in life, and gone down the Nile or somewhere exotic."

Harry laughed. Then he saw the scowl creep across her face. "You're serious, I take it." Of course she was, he chided himself. When he was young and optimistic, he too believed that marriage would fill the holes in his life. Now, he just wanted to feel a sense of passion again.

"I certainly am. I wanted more experiences before I settled down in this grey little world."

He wondered why she had married Lawrence with beliefs such as these. Perhaps she had been forced. Or maybe it had seemed right at that time, and now that she was married she wondered why she was.

"People treat women like they don't have brains. I don't know why I can't have an opinion about things."

"I suspect it always has been that way."

"Perhaps it is time to treat women as if they are people rather than belongings. We're not chattel."

"True." She really was liberal, he thought. She wasn't like the other women he knew.

"Why are my possessions my husband's now that we have married?" She certainly didn't beat about the bush or mince her words.

He didn't really know the answer to that. He had never thought about the unfairness of it before. He moved closer to her. She wasn't like the other women he knew.

A bird trilled a long high note. He wondered what kind of bird it might be.

She reached out and touched his cheekbones lightly as if she were wiping away a speck of dirt. His throat hurt.

He wished the two of them could stay frozen in this moment. He let his fingertips move across her mouth for a long second.

Something or somebody crashed in the woods behind them. Lawrence's uniquely grating voice called, "Octavia?"

She jumped up, turning away from Harry. "Here, I am." She moved hastily towards Lawrence's voice.

Harry wondered if Lawrence had seen them, but he didn't really care. The soft promise in her words sent him over the edge. Maybe life was offering him a second chance at love in the temporal world.

After Harry's wife died, his way of life—his world—shifted. He had struggled to become father and mother to their three-year-old daughter, Martha. And then within six months she died too. That was when he had turned to the Jesuits. The peace and predictability of that world intrigued him. Unexpected events such as sudden illness did not take place there as easily because any changes that occurred were expected to occur. The ringing of the bells signaled the movement of time; one day became like the next as the seasons came and went: activity, prayer and meditation, meal and then activity again. The rituals satisfied him. The monks clearly had work to do, and they seemed enthusiastic about it. He found a quiet passion to his life again – there was joy in his life again. But his father needed him back in his law office. Gold from the Klondike strike in 1897 was flowing into the banks, providing a basis for credit and economic expansion. Companies were earning fortunes in railway, retailing, steel and oil. So Harry donned his stiffly laundered collars and cuffs and dutifully reported back to the dusty law offices and his life of quiet desperation two years ago.

Once July came, Harry fled the hot New York streets for Stockbridge. He picnicked and drove through the countryside with a tea basket loaded with delicacies and some lovely young nieces of his aging bridge partners. He brushed off their chattering advances and wondered what the monks were doing. He attended the archery parties, met simpering debutantes at tennis parties, doffed his stiff round straw hat at all the women as he walked the quiet streets of the village, and had even taken the occasional expedition to Lebanon in the livery stable's one four-in-hand with several handsome – but oh so boring – women. Throughout this entire summer, Harry hadn't done anything or met anyone who sent any passionate frissons up and down his spine. He missed his wife, but she had died so long ago that he had a hard time remembering what she looked like.

A crow called. Harry picked up her hat off the log. He tossed it into the air. Maybe life wouldn't be so boring anymore. When he walked back to the game, she had gone. His friend Paul looked at him and shrugged. Harry smiled. At least he had her hat. He stroked its jaunty feather. Later that day he took his favorite horse out for a long gallop in Stockbridge Bowl.

That night, the moon turned the mountain ranges from fluid lavender to massive black. The stars were reflected in the lake. He went to the dance, where he saw Octavia standing somewhat apart from a group of heavily corseted women. He danced with his mother and with Paul's wife, and then swept Octavia off in a waltz. Clinging to him and shutting her eyes, she danced with him. He could feel her warm body through his fingers. He felt full with longing. Her husband entered the room just as the waltz was ending. Harry's fingers tightened. Her eyes opened and she saw Lawrence, who cocked a fierce eyebrow at her. Her face paled. "Harry, I must go." She walked unsteadily toward Lawrence, who pulled her out of the room.

They did not return.

A light rain blanketed the gently rolling Berkshires the following morning. The center of the village was busier than Harry had ever seen it. Small groups of people huddled in front of the post office. Bicyclists and horse-drawn wagons were milling about on the street. He sat quietly for a few seconds, studying the scene.

His friend Paul stopped him. "Have you heard?"

"Heard what?"

"About Lawrence's wife."

"Octavia. What about her." This used to be such a comfortable, self-contained, well-regulated little world, Harry thought.

"She went for a late night swim in the lake and drowned. What a crazy thing to do."

The sounding of the church bell was clear and steady. Perhaps, Harry thought, it was time for him to return to the monastery where he had found joy before. Maybe that joy would last.

The Heartbroken Chauffeur

Chauffer John Widders was a happy man. He lived in North Adams, a flourishing mill town, during the early 1900s. He knew the familiar sweetness of knowing what to do at every hour of every day. He wasn't responsible for making the decisions; he just had to carry them out. A bachelor with few close friends, he cared for the Houghton cars and the Houghton family.

A large imposing man, Widders was employed by Albert C. Houghton, who had served as the first mayor of North Adams. President of the former Arnold Print Works, he had built a large, three-story Victorian mansion in the late 1890s, where he lived with his wife, Cordelia, and their daughter, Mary. A younger daughter had died earlier.

Widders doted on the Houghton family, especially Mary. Blonde and hazel-eyed, she would bring him her broken toys to fix; they would work together to give the doll a new arm or leg. As she grew older, she would rescue the hurt bird or the wounded rabbit and attempt to nurse them back to health. Widders and she would make shoebox hospitals and she would keep her patients in the garage, where he cared for the Houghton cars. One day when she was trying to feed a rabbit with a broken leg, Mary said, "You know, Widders, what I want to be?"

"A good girl," he laughed.

"Widders, I already am a good girl. That's not funny."

"I'm sorry, Miss Mary. I was just kidding you."

"I want to help others."

"And how would you do that?" he asked, stopping his polishing of the hood.

"I'd like to be a nurse in order to relieve the suffering in the world."

Widders knew that her mother had bigger ambitions for her pretty daughter than working in a hospital, but he said, "That's a good ambition for you to have, Miss Mary."

Mary spent a lot of time talking to Widders. He didn't dismiss her or tell her to change her clothes and get ready for dinner or school or church. He just listened patiently to her stories about school, friends, dances, and the family. His garage was his castle. He was fierce in his protection of the Houghton family and devoted to their welfare. Their happiness gave his life meaning.

When she became a teen, she began to talk about her feelings with him. "Have you ever wanted to laugh when there is no reason to, Widders?"

"Not so that I've noticed, Miss Mary."

"Sometimes I do. This year the sun is so bright and the birds so loud that I awake at dawn and I feel like dancing… I feel like running in the meadow and falling on the grass and smelling the lilies in bloom."

"You're growing up, Miss Mary."

Widders was saving for retirement. He figured that when Mary left home he might move on. While he was making his plans and saving his money, though, a terrible life-changing event happened.

On August 1, 1911, a beautiful summer day, the Houghtons, with their friend Sybil Hutton, decided to go to Vermont for dinner. Widders drove the family and their guests in the big Pierce-Arrow touring car, and everyone was enjoying the rolling Vermont hills and the peaceful farms. When they approached the steep Pownal Center Hill, Widders saw workmen on the road and a team of horses approaching. He swerved to avoid the horses and came too close to the road's left shoulder. The gravel shoulder collapsed, and the car rolled down the embankment, turning over three times. The car roof crushed and killed Sybil; Mary Houghton was pronounced dead a few hours later. Both John Widders and Mr. Houghton only had minor injuries.

As the shocked town grieved, Widders blamed himself. No one else did. He wasn't charged with any crime, but he had adored Mary and he was at the wheel of the car when she died. One day, he walked into a barn behind the large, three-story mansion and shot himself.

Mr. Houghton never fully recovered, emotionally, from the tragedy. He died soon after the accident — some say from overwhelming despair. His widow lived seven more sad and lonely years in the house, dying in 1918.

Ghost hunters are still looking for the residents of this three-story Victorian mansion.

Ownership was passed to the Gallup family in 1918. They quickly sold the property to the local Masonic Lodge, which still owns the building. In 1920, the Masons added an extensive lodge and anterooms at the rear of the mansion.

Although Widders joined the Houghtons in the family burial plot, North Adams residents say that Widders still hasn't passed over. Many times over the years, people have heard ghostly footsteps in the building, but no spirit has been seen.

Since the Masons acquired the property, there have been rumors of strange happenings in the mansion. In 1993, three maintenance workers were supposedly taking a lunch break on the second floor when they heard heavy footsteps on the stairs. They searched downstairs, but there was no one else in the mansion. This was not a unique occurrence—people have reported hearing such footsteps a number of times over the years. Others have reported hearing steps on the stairs leading to the third floor, where John Widders once slept. These slow heavy footsteps suggest to many that the heartbroken chauffeur still hasn't forgiven himself. People have reported feeling an icy blast of air on the stairs as the unforgiving spirit of Chauffer John Widders passes by, heading up the stairs as he once headed up the fateful hill.

Others have experienced a range of unexplained phenomena, including loud banging on doors and walls, inexplicable cold spots in certain rooms, and intermittent problems using cell phones. The basement and the third floor seem to be particular trouble spots; strange voices have been heard in both areas. Some have reported seeing a light on the third floor, which has no working light, and of seeing someone through the window there when no one was in the building. Interestingly enough, no phenomena have occurred in the new wing.

Still in use as a Masonic Temple today, the house is maintained by the Lafayette Graylock Masonic Lodge A.F. & A.M.

and the Naomi Chapter of the Eastern Star — non-profit organizations that support charities. Interestingly enough, when people leave the main house and enter the temple, many are suddenly filled with a feeling of peace. There have been no significant reports of paranormal activity in this newer section of the building.

Some believe that when tragic events occur, something may be left behind, lingering around the place where the suffering took place. Berkshire Paranormal Group, which has its headquarters in the mansion, has definitely detected paranormal activity in the mansion. They have recorded erratic, inconsistent EMF readings and captured orbs simultaneously on digital.

The Mosstream Phantom

Whenever he went down town,
We people on the pavement looked at him:
He was a gentleman from sole to crown,
Clean favored, and imperially slim.

And he was always quietly arrayed,
And he was always human when he talked;

But still he fluttered pulses when he said,
"Good-morning," and he glittered when he walked.

And he was rich - yes, richer than a king -
And admirably schooled in every grace;
In fine we thought that he was everything
To make us wish that we were in his place.

Edwin Arlington Robinson

Ghostly residents still wander about Berkshires' elegant old mansions. One of these is the not-so-small cottage called Mosstream. Andrew Rigby built Mosstream in the early part of the twentieth century for his summer residence and studio.

Tall and darkly handsome, Andrew Rigby had a distinguished background. His ancestors included a famous explorer and a signer of the Declaration of Independence. After graduating from Harvard in the late nineteenth century, he went abroad to study painting and sculpture in Paris and Florence. He had the money to live well. Like many artists during that time, he stayed in Europe for over a decade, exhibiting works and winning many medals — both there and back in the United States.

Mr. Rigby made four graceful statues for Atlanta's opera house. Among his more famous paintings is "The Left Bank," for which he received a medal at the International Exposition in Berlin in 1891. Another painting, "A Woman's Woman," is in the permanent collection at the Museum of Fine Arts in Boston. The King of Norway personally presented him with a medal of honor for "The Elegant Woman," a figure in bronze, which can be found in one of Philadelphia's more prestigious museums.

Yes, the impeccably tailored and groomed Andrew Rigby was an important man. In New York, his large fireplaced studio replicated a room in an ancient French monastery and occupied the northeast wing of his New York City mansion. Its walls were covered with exquisite tapestries from Morocco and Spain. Visitors could watch Mr. Rigby paint from the balcony. He was a much-envied man.

Each summer, he would take his wife, Alice, and his children, Anna, John, and Belinda to their summer cottage in the piney woods of the Berkshires, where they could retire in unabashed opulence for six weeks during the heat of the summer.

His summer cottage was like many summerhouses in the Berkshires: a substantial mansion as a shrine to his success. Sited on more than one hundred acres, the house was designed by a famous architect. Talented craftsmen were employed to carve the wood, to bend the copper, and to cast the iron, and Alice and the architect went all over New York visiting every antique, decorator, and similar shops to find the right piece of furniture or china.

According to Mr. Rigby's wishes, Mosstream was rustic in spirit. Rough-hewn stone steps led from the patio to the terrace; the grounds were left wild rather than cleared for gardens. Despite his formidable ancestry, he believed a man should show his roots. The central hall was the focus of the house. The oak paneled walls were covered with tapestries, the pocket doors were massive, and the hardwood floors were stained dark. The principal public rooms – the dining room, the library, and the drawing room – flowed from there. Inglenooks, bays, and alcoves allowed quieter activities. Four of the six fireplaces were made of Carrara marble. There was one enclosed porch on the north side, and another on the south side.

The library had a Tudor ceiling with a large bronze chandelier; the dining room was paneled in quartered oak. His bedroom (in those days couples often slept separately) had a parquet floor and a fireplace with a mantel of Carrara marble. Alice's bedroom had walls covered in pink satin and quantities of lace. The third floor consisted of six bedrooms for the help and two baths. The wine cellar held two thousand bottles of great vintages.

The family brought some household servants with them: the butler, cook, and a lady's maid. They hired locals, who considered themselves fortunate to get the work; they carried coal to the fireplaces, swept the dusty grates daily, loaded the dumbwaiters, and mowed acres of lawns. A laundress was in charge of the massive laundry; a kitchen maid assisted the cook, a chambermaid was upstairs, and a parlor maid, downstairs.

Yes, Mr. Rigby had a good life. He had a wife and three children, two houses, servants, a good career, and sometimes he even had an audience in his New York studio to watch him paint. Having the good life, however, does not mean the absence of temptation…

Some former servants have said that one year the Rigbys brought a pretty Welsh girl named Anghorad from New York to work as the parlor maid. She was a lovely person with a way of gazing at you through her clear blue eyes that made you feel like the most important person in the world. She had a rose and cream complexion, a sparkle in her eyes, and a skip in her step. But sometimes she was caught sobbing for her family and her friends back in Wales.

When you are homesick for your family and friends, you can become vulnerable to the kind word, to the affectionate pat, to the admiring look in your master's eye. Suddenly, you are susceptible, and you do those things that you ought not to if you are just a powerless parlor maid. Yes, Anghorad is said to have become pregnant … and lost the sparkle in her eye.

Several months later the pregnancy was no more, and she died suddenly. No one knows who the father was or who botched the abortion. Mr. Rigby, with his knowledge of European practices, is said to have been her lover and murderer. Her body was found in the laundry room, but that is all that is known.

After Mr. Rigby died in 1920, the estate was sold several times. During this time, people realized that the property included a ghost. The villagers reported hearing someone moaning or crying. People talked about seeing a beautiful young face in the laundry room window.

Over the years, the house was refurbished as houses often are. The massive floral wallpapers were stripped off; the walls were painted; electric lights replaced gaslights; and the plumbing was modernized. The hall still remained dark when the pocket doors were closed, but sometimes the doors, all by themselves, would begin to slide in and out of their pockets. Then the sounds began. Loud knocks would hammer on doors, but no one would be there. Doors would slam, and an odd moaning would be heard. Not a window would be open, but there would be a whisper of cold air as though a ghost had just slipped past. Some ghost hunters say that their security cameras caught a wraithlike woman's figure coming down the hall. Then the figure would suddenly melt away.

Of course, people talk, especially when people are famous, and stories about the rich and famous get exaggerated. Is this story true? We may never know.

What we do know is that the town records don't mention a Welsh parlor maid named Anghorad, but perhaps she was only a poor Welsh girl who slipped into this country. We also know a woman's cries are often heard up and down the halls of Moss-tream. Some of us may not believe in the afterlife, but perhaps when some people die they leave an imprint — a faint disturbance of energy that can be sensed by later generations.

The Legacy

Once upon a time, her grandmother's home was her favorite place to be. It was so distinctive with its well-proportioned spaces and good light. Porches, bays, and towers opened up the interior; the exterior was covered with cedar shingles in various patterns. But today, on her visit here after all these years, the large rambling shingle-style house lurked behind leafless trees, which blew in a chilled wind. It looked so gloomy.

After her grandmother died, Laura inherited the house. Newly engaged to Michael, Laura couldn't afford to pay the taxes, and she certainly didn't want to live eighty minutes from the city. She was the only family member remaining. After meeting with her grandmother's accountant, Laura quickly contracted with local realtors to sell the house and called in an appraiser. It was all hers, after all. The American, European, and the Far Eastern furniture, ceramics, and artwork belonged to her, but she really didn't want them. Hat racks, a lady's dressing table, Chippendale sofas, and parlor chairs didn't fit into her life. So she sold them all.

The house sold quickly. The prospective owners, the O'Brien's, wanted the two large gilt-framed paintings of Laura's aunts that hung in the front hall. They thought they looked really handsome there. Mrs. O'Brien laughed and said, "I would love to have these two beauties be my ancestors."

Mr. O'Brien added, "Their contrasting colors and their poses certainly add to your new relatives' attractiveness, my dear."

"We'll give you twenty percent above their appraised cost," Mrs. O'Brien said.

Laura had never known her aunts – for some never-explained reason the women in her family didn't get along – and they had died long before she realized that she could reach out to them on her own. But Laura had liked the portraits.

Both oils were quite beautiful. Great Aunt Judith had her hair smoothed back in a dark knot, her low-necked, red rose dress draped to perfection, cut to make the most of her less-than-impressive bosom. A delicate multi-stone diamond necklace circled her throat. Great Aunt Marie was a brown-eyed, tawny blond in a blue silk shirt. She looked seductively at the viewer, pointing with one dainty finger at the large oval emerald pendant around her neck.

When she was young, Laura used to talk to them. She would make up stories about the two women, whom she called Snow White and Rose Red. Without any sisters or brothers, she had no one to talk to when she visited. She would sit and play with her dolls in front of them. As she grew older, she would pretend that they nodded in agreement or smiled approvingly at her stories. The lawyer told her that her grandmother had been found in the great hall underneath the massive portrait of her Aunt Judith. She had a terrified look on her face, but there was no sign of forced entry.

She knew, however, a second floor walk up on the West Side was no place for two, four-foot gilt-framed portraits. So she sold them to the O'Briens. She had also sold the necklace and the pendant that she had found in Grandmother's leather jewelry box. She wouldn't ever be in a position to wear diamonds or an emerald pendant. When she and Michael married, she used the proceeds, along with the money from the sale of the house, to buy a hundred-year-old cottage for Michael and her. It had been a guesthouse on the estate of a landmark Shingle style house, which was one of several dozen large Shingle style homes that formed a private summer community of well-to-do Bostonians. Built in the style of its venerable neighbors, the cottage allowed them to enjoy the setting year-round.

Over the years, she and Michael did quite well. They never did have any children, but they had each other. They worked, held an annual holiday party in their small cottage, collected Blue Willow pottery, and focused on their shade garden of hosta, ferns, and cimicifuga. They treated the plants like children, searching for ones whose flowers ranged from delicately diminutive to exotic, those with intriguing foliage, and those with forms that stand out in a winter garden. When Michael died, Laura realized how alone she was. No children, no aunts, no cousins. All she had was just a lot of Blue Willow pottery, several award-winning shade gardens, and a small cottage.

She was very lonely. She would hoard the funny story, the gossipy tidbit all day just waiting to share it and then realize that there was no one to listen. When she went out, there was no one to look at her significantly, signaling, "Hey, it's time to get out of here." When she entered the house, only her dog greeted her. She realized if she were to fall down the basement stairs and lie there in a pool of blood, it might be several days before someone knew she was missing.

Michael was no longer around to discuss whether they should divide this hosta or not, to discuss what to have for dinner, or whether they should go to the upcoming auction. He couldn't tell her whether she looked good when she went to church or to the symphony. She found that she couldn't even put on her favorite necklace without him to help out with the difficult catch. She wondered if she was beginning to smell musty and old.

Three months after Michael had died, Laura decided she had to do something or go see a therapist. She decided to visit the village where her grandmother had lived. She would search for her roots. She knew the O'Briens had sold the house. Who lived there now? What was it like now that the town had become so famous during the summer? So she wrote a letter, introducing herself and asking for an invitation. The new owner called in three days. Come for a drink, she said.

A single light gleamed from the downstairs window as Laura pulled into the driveway. There was the octagonal-shaped screened porch where she had learned to jump rope and the oak front door with stained glass panels. She pulled the old brass knocker and was greeted by the newest owner, Mrs. Hillary, a slim, stony-faced woman in a cashmere cardigan and plaid wool skirt. "So you're Laura. Please come in."

Laura glanced around the great hall, which included a large fireplace, the graciously ascending principal staircase, and a great wall of windows. The hall was the informal center point of a home created expressly many years ago as a country estate. The suite of principal ground floor rooms – the hall, parlor, dining room, and library – were arranged so that they could be opened to each other by sliding aside great pairs of oaken doors into wall pockets. As a child, she used to love sliding the great doors back into their nooks.

She could see that the hall, parlor, dining room, and library were carpeted in Oriental rugs in red and blue tones. The furniture was suitably massive. "Thank you. It's getting chilly out there."

"It is, but we have a fire. We can sit there, and you can get warm."

"That would be nice." Laura felt awkward. "It's such a cold damp day."

"I want to talk to you about something."

"Oh?"

"I feel like I've known you for such a long time," Mrs. Hillary added.

"But we have never met." Laura thought she heard a laugh from somewhere in the house. "Oh, is someone else here?"

"No, it's just you and me … but I have your relatives here." She pointed behind Laura. "And they make themselves felt."

Laura looked behind her. There hung Great Aunts Marie and Judith. "Oh," she gasped. "My great aunts. Everyone else is dead – except for me – and they are still here. I was so sure they would have been sold."

"Oh, no. The O'Briens said they belonged to the house and that they should stay with it." Her laughter was hollow.

Laura raised an eyebrow. Mrs. Hillary looked ordinary enough, but she certainly was somewhat strange. "Why did they think that?"

"The O'Briens said it was their house after all, so they should let them keep it. That taking them would be like kicking them out."

"Oh that's interesting, but what do you think?"

"Well, sometimes I wonder if they would be happier somewhere else."

"Really?" Laura's heart jumped. She would have a family again. Two beautiful aunts painted in oils. Rose Red and Snow White would be back in her life — someone she could talk to.

"They are your relatives, so they would be better off with you."

Laura was suddenly reminded of her mother debating whether she should care for her grandmother as she became elderly or send her to an assisted living home. But her mother had died, so her grandmother had stayed where she wanted to be—right here. "Oh that's amazing. You want me to take them — to my house." The big gold-framed portraits would look rather overwhelming in her cottage. They certainly wouldn't go with her patchwork quilt interior either. But they were family after all.

"Yes, I know they would be happier with you."

"Really?"

"Well, it sounds odd, I know, but sometimes I hear this rustling — like silk dresses and no one is here…" Her voice trailed off.

Laura didn't really know what to say to that comment. "You know," she laughed, "when I was a little girl I used to think of them as Rose Red and Snow White. I never knew them. They were just these two beautiful women who my grandmother would never talk about." She was babbling, she thought.

Mrs. Hillary's lips tightened. "You should take them. They are your relatives after all."

"You mean, like, today?"

"Yes. My husband says I'm crazy to give them to you, but he doesn't have to live with them." Mrs. Hillary's hands waved frantically.

Laura stood under the two portraits. "Hmm." That was odd, she thought. Aunt Marie certainly had a haunting stare; her eyes seemed to follow her. Laura shook her head. She was thinking crazy. That portrait must have a crack in its veneer.

Mrs. Hillary said, "Stay here dear. Sit right here so you can see the portraits. I'll go get a stepladder. Mustn't waste time." She seemed relieved.

Laura wasn't sure where she would put them, but she wasn't going to lose this opportunity to acquire a family.

Mrs. Hillary patted a Lincoln rocker. "Sit down. Let me get us a glass of something to drink, and then we can sit in front of the fire. Will sherry do?" She bustled out of the room.

"Oh you really shouldn't bother," Laura said to her back, but she really wanted a glass of something. She was feeling rather odd. It was almost as if she was being watched, but of course the house was so old it probably did have a ghost or two. She heard a creak and felt a whisper of movement. Old houses often creak, she told herself. Heating pipes make noise.

Had Aunt Judith just blinked? She felt she had just missed seeing a flicker of her eyelids. As she stared at the beautiful face, she began to think that Aunt Judith was moving. Impossible, she thought, the portrait was only an inanimate object.

Aunts Judith and Marie looked down at her. She felt rather dowdy compared to them. They were so glamorous. She would have someone to talk with again. She wouldn't be so alone.

She glanced toward the fireplace, which was throwing strange shadows on the walls. The clock ticked. Was something moving behind her back? There was a strange stillness in the air. Her shoulder was touched by something, but it was only a billowing drape in a room where there wasn't any air.

Laura shook her head. The radiators whistled; the windows rattled in the wind. Then she heard a slight rustling sound as though something was stirring. She felt the crawl of goose-flesh on her neck. With it came a smell, a stifling smell of wet ground, dead leaves and decay. What was Mrs. Hillary doing for so long?

Marie seemed to be glaring at her. Her breath began to shudder. There was no air in the room. The rustling seemed to be louder. Something that felt like wire tightened around her neck. A low voice said, "We belong here." The clock ticked, and a fierce gust of wind blew through the room. "This is our house. You sold everything else."

The Dancing Shoes

Some ghost stories, such as this one, are quite familiar. I heard this one on my first ghost tour of the Berkshires.

Daylight was waning as the girl with long blond hair approached the circle of dancers, swirling and twirling, around the bonfire. The music ebbed and rose, ebbed and rose. The dancers made a wide circle and began to move, swaying and humming, bending and clapping. The wind carried their hair streaming out behind them.

The sunset crimsoned the hills beyond. She watched, the tears sliding down her cheeks to her black lace top. She cried because her sweetheart had died in an automobile accident six months ago. She had been with him, but she wasn't hurt. He had been driving too fast – probably because of the martinis he had drank – and plowed right into a tree. She had screamed as the branches came closer and closer, but they bent when they came into contact with her.

After the funeral, everyone returned to her apartment for a farewell drink. His friends crowded the small apartment and nosily drank beer as they told stories about him: the time when he threw a gazing ball from the overpass and it hit a car, the first dance, the first car accident... When they all left, she put on his old navy sweatshirt with his familiar smell and hung his shirts and pants in the closet. That night, when she went to bed, the blankets remained smooth on his side of the bed. She was alone, but he couldn't leave.

She had lived as a hermit since the accident. She never went out. She never returned her phone calls. She never went with her friends who danced and partied almost every night. The only place she went was to the cemetery, where she sat crying by his grave.

In the evenings, the children would play flashlight tag or catch fireflies in a jar within the friendly confines of the yard, while the adults rocked in their chairs, telling stories, watching the stars, even singing some songs. And slowly the lights of the night would turn on, and she would know – once again – that she was alone.

But the month came when the moon was just beginning to shiver in the sky. The cornfields had turned into brown stubble and the maple trees bright yellow and something lured her out to the unusually warm late September night.

She had donned her black spiky heels that night and gone to where her friends were dancing. But tonight next to the fire she was alone. Everyone else was paired up, two by two. A Noah's Ark scene, yet she was a single.

She lifted her eyes and focused on the wavering flames of the fire. Suddenly, one of the couples broke from the group and started turning and whirling. Others followed, flinging their arms out, uttering shrill cries. The area was fraught with passion

Down the road came a lone car. Out stepped a tall man from the flickering shadows. The dancers came to a sudden stop. Talking quietly, they picked up their belongings and left.

The man stood over the girl. "Why are you crying?" he asked.

Shifting her position so she could better see his face in the faint moonlight, she sobbed, "I'm crying for my sweetheart."

"But it is time for you to come back to life and live again."

"But he's not here," she wailed.

"Is that true?" His deep murmur stirred the fine hairs at her nape.

She looked up and saw her sweetheart, his eyes twinkling. He reached out a hand. "Come dance with me. I'm not going to let you go tonight. But I have to be home by daylight."

And they danced as they never danced before. His embrace was so warm that she would swear she could smell smoke. He kissed her eyes, her nose, and her lips again and again; she reciprocated with furious joy in the thick blanketing darkness.

The night went on, and they went on as only lovers can. Branches swayed and creaked, and things you couldn't see rustled and snapped in the dark.

As the birds began to rustle and the grey chilly dawn to appear out of the midnight blackness, he pulled away, saying, "I have to go."

"No," she said. "I'm not going to let you leave me again."

"But you must! I can't cross over as long as you carry on this way."

"No, no, no! I'm not leaving you again." She jumped into his red car, dropping her black spiky heels in the back seat. "See you can't get rid of me."

Grimfaced, he got into the driver's seat and started the car. She felt cold and damp. The night grew paler as he drove on. He stopped at a cemetery.

"Come." He pulled her out of the car.

"But my shoes," she protested.

"Leave the shoes."

"The grass is cold."

"So am I," he snapped.

He dragged her barefoot through the overgrown grass to his grave. The grass brushed her legs. It was still and silent in the chill dawn. She wished a bird would sing, but not even a crow called.

"This is where I live now," he said, "but I can't have any rest with your weeping and wailing and staying home like a hermit. It's time for me to leave, and your sorrow has me tied tight. If you insist on this, come with me to my grave."

She began to pull away. "No, no," she cried.

"It's the only way," he said.

"No," she screamed, and she began to run in her bare feet across the frosty grass. The sun was looming over the horizon by the time she arrived home in her bare feet.

This graveyard is not as quiet as it appears.

She felt cold to the bone for almost a week. Then, she returned to the cemetery. She passed the ancient gravestones engraved with skulls and the newer gravestones decorated with urns. She came to his gravestone, and there her black spiky heels were waiting.

The Two Canoes

The Native American tales from the area have been told and retold. Here is yet another telling…

The jewel of the Berkshires is often said to be Pontoosuc Lake in Pittsfield. Many years ago, the Mohegan Indians called it the Shoon-keek-Moon-keek Lake.

On a still moonless night in the area near Pittsfield, you may hear the plaintive cry "Shoon-keek?" across the quiet Pontoosuc

Lake and the response, "Moon-keek," echo back from the silent surrounding hill.

Three hundred years before the Europeans came to the region, two brothers settled around the lake now known as Pontoosuc. One brother had a daughter named Moon-keek. The other had a son called Shoon-keek. The two children grew up together, playing in the forest, scrambling under the tangle of grapevines, alders, and red dogwood to find their special hiding spots. Shoon-keek's keen eyes would find a trail marked with deer hooves leading to higher land, and they would climb to the high cliffs. They would lie on the mossy forest carpet under groves of beeches alive with squirrels and bird song. They would watch the beavers build their lodges and the squirrels hide their acorns. They would swim in the beautiful lake, canoe around its edge, and fish in the crystal clear streams.

And as in all stories such as this, he grew strong and she grew beautiful. They were each other's best friend.

Now, the law of all Indian tribes forbids cousins from marrying, and these two were first cousins. Meanwhile, there was another brave, Nockawando, who wanted to marry Moon-keek. She resisted his overtures, so he went to her father, saying that Moon-keek was too familiar with Shoon-keek and that they were disobeying tribal customs. He argued that first cousins should not permitted to be together.

Her father agreed and went to his brother. Together, they agreed that Moon-keek and Shoon-keek had to be separated. This relationship could not continue.

But like many young couples, this young couple resisted their parents' attempt to part them. They would sneak out and meet whenever they could. They met on the mountaintops, in the forests, and in the valleys. They used their birch bark canoes for transportation, finding secluded spots and islands on the perimeter of the lake. Every day they met, and every day they were a little bolder with each other. Finally, they decided to leave the area and ask another tribe to adopt them. They planned to meet at one of their favorite islands—and they promised to meet beneath the lake, if anything interfered with their flight.

> *By the shores of Gitche Gumee,*
> *By the shining Big-Sea-Water,*
> *Stood the wigwam of Nokomis,*
> *Daughter of the Moon, Nokomis.*
> *Dark behind it rose the forest,*
> *Rose the black and gloomy pine-trees,*
> *Rose the firs with cones upon them;*
> *Bright before it beat the water,*
> *Beat the clear and sunny water,*
> *Beat the shining Big-Sea-Water.*
> *Song of Hiawatha, Henry Wadsworth Longfellow*

The night on which they planned to leave, the jealous Nocka-wando was spying on Moon-keek, afraid that she would leave the tribe. He watched her leave her father's lodge and silently walk to her canoe and paddle to a distant island. He then went to Shoon-keek's lodge and watched him quietly leave his father's lodge and board his canoe. Nockawando got into his canoe and paddled softly after Shoon-keek. When Nockawando was within range, he shot Shoon-keek with an arrow. The young lover fell into the dark lake waters.

But his canoe continued on and on — as if paddled by an invisible spirit. When it swiftly passed the island where Moon-keek waited, she had a premonition about the events that had occurred. She leapt into her own canoe and pushed out from shore. Nockawando heard her raise her death-song and paddled as rapidly as he could, but near the middle of the lake his arms stopped paddling as if gripped by a stronger force than he.

The night became strangely still. There wasn't even the sound of the loon or a rustle of a leaf. He watched as she called out, "Shoon-keek? Shoon-keek?" The lake answered, "Moon-keek… Moon-keek…" As Nockawando watched, Moon-keek slipped quietly into the lake, and the waters closed gently over her head. Her canoe glided on to join Shoon-keek's empty canoe.

The next day, the Indians looked for their bodies, but they were never found. The Indians believed, however, that they were together, paddling their birch bark canoes.

On the nights when the moon rises from the water, the Indians often see the two canoes skimming the waters of the lake, sometimes together, sometimes a little apart — but not very far. Sometimes they heard the cry "Moon-keek" and the answer "Shoon-keek." And so they named the lake after these two who would not be parted.

DIRECTIONS: Pontoosuc Lake is a recreation area in the Berkshires of Western Massachusetts. The 480-acre lake borders Lanesborough and Pittsfield, Massachusetts.

The Spirit of Bash Bish Falls

Waterfalls make many sounds. They bubble, slosh, gurgle, chortle, splash, murmur, ripple, babble, and even lap against the rocks. Some say that Bash Bish Falls says its name over and over: bashbish, bashbish, bashbish. When you visit, see if you can hear it.

Bash Bish Falls, tucked away in the southwest corner of the Berkshires, is not only the state's highest waterfall but it is a twin fall that begins with a series of cascades twisting through a deep gorge until the water meets a large granite outcrop, which then splits it into two fifty-foot cataracts tumbling into a clear green mountain pool. After the drama of the falls, Bash Bish Brook continues through New York State until it finally joins the Hudson River on its way to the Atlantic.

A popular Berkshires tourist stop, Bash Bish Falls has been a favorite subject of painters and photographers since the mid-nineteenth century. Most visitors stay at the lower twin falls and rock-bottomed basin. Only the braver attempt to explore the upper reaches of the multiple falls.

A long time before the English began exploring North America, a lovely Mohegan woman, called Bash Bish, lived in a village near the falls with her husband and daughter. Everyone liked her because she was so much fun to be with — everyone but one, who professed to be her friend. Of course, like many of us who never imagine that we could have an enemy disguised as a friend, Bash Bish didn't realize that her jealous friend planned to hurt her.

And she did — one day her friend accused her of having a love affair with a man other than her husband. In front of the tribal council, Bash Bish begged, cried, and pled her innocence, holding out her infant daughter, asking, "How can you accuse me? You're my friend."

"But you are guilty of breaking tribal laws," sneered her enemy. "You deserve to die."

The laws of the tribe were harsh, and the village council condemned her to death by water. They planned to tie her in a canoe and launch it upstream.

That morning, the air was cold and still. All the tribe members were quiet. The small animals scurried deep into the forest. As the Indians tied her into the canoe and placed it into the water, the rays of the sun shone all around her, creating a golden aura, and multihued butterflies rose like winged blessings. The Indians were awestruck. Was Bash Bish a witch? A spirit?

The canoe with her strapped in it plunged over the falls. Downstream, the Indians retrieved the broken canoe, but much to their astonishment her body had disappeared.

Later, people said they could see her spirit shimmering in the water, but many people forgot about her unless they had been there the day when the butterflies flew.

An old squaw adopted Bash Bish's baby. She named her White Swan because she was so fair. As she grew, she became more beautiful each day. She was so lovely that the Chief, Black Thunder, picked White Swan as a bride for his son, Whirling Wind.

For many months, these two happily roamed the beautiful Berkshire woods while Whirling Wind demonstrated his hunting skills to his lovely bride. He could bring down moose, deer, and even bear with his bow and arrow. She would run along the trail behind her husband. Sometimes she would join him in fishing for salmon and trout. They would sit for hours while he told her about his adventures with the tribe on the warpath. In the evening, they would sit and listen to the whispering of the pine trees and watch the fireflies flitting through the evening's dusk. Although White Swan and Whirling Wind were a devoted couple, they had one great sadness. She was unable to conceive.

Now, Whirling Wind was Black Thunder's only son and heir. When Black Thunder died, Whirling Wind would be the chief. He also had to have a son and heir. The young couple visited the Medicine Man who brewed many different potions and performed dances by the light of the mystic fire deep in the forest, but still White Swan did not get pregnant.

Finally, Black Thunder announced that Whirling Wind must take another squaw to his wigwam — one who would give him an heir. Reluctantly, Whirling Wind took a second wife. Although White Swan understood the reasons why this must be done, she was not happy. Her glowing smile no longer brightened the wigwam. She no longer happily followed her husband up the trail or sat in the front of his birch bark canoe. Instead, they slowly and silently trodded the path to the high rock above the falls. There, she would sit and watch the plummeting waters. Sometimes when Whirling Wind left the village, he could hear her talking to the spirit, which all Indians knew lived in the plunging cascade.

One night when the moon was full, White Swan rose from her couch and left Whirling Wind's wigwam. He watched her go and then quietly followed her, but she was a good deal faster than he. She ran like a deer along the path, over the slippery rocks, to the high rock on which she sat and watched the falls.

Fearfully, Whirling Wind called to her as he tried to jump over the treacherous rocks over which she had skimmed like the bird for whom she had been named. He could hear the water splashing below. Breathless, he arrived at the base of the falls, just as she stepped onto the highest rock above. He was just in time to hear her cry, "Hear I am, Mother; take me into your arms," and she disappeared into the water. The waters roiled briefly and a beautiful white mist rose up. Desperate, Whirling Wind dove after her and succumbed to the tumult.

The Indians found Whirling Wind's battered body, but they never found White Swan's, which, like that of her mother's, disappeared. Some say that the voices of these two women can be heard in the waterfall's gurgling. Others say that they can see White Swan's face, formed by the swirling waters at the base of the falls, looking upward to the spot where she and her husband plunged to their deaths.

DIRECTIONS: From Mass. Pike (I-90), take Exit 2 in Lee. Follow Mass. Route 102 west for 4.7 miles to Stockbridge. Turn left and follow U.S. Route 7 south for 7.7 miles through Great Barrington. Turn right and follow Mass. Route 23 west for 4.9 miles to South Egremont. Turn left onto Mass. Route 41 south, then take immediate right, Mount Washington Road; continue for 7.5 miles (becomes East Street). Turn right onto Cross Road, then right onto West Street and continue for one mile. Turn left onto Falls Road and follow for 1.5 miles to parking lot and trailhead on left.

Cascading water tumbles over gorges and drops over eighty feet into a sparkling pool at Bash Bish Waterfall. *Courtesy of Robert D. Evans.*

Legend of Monument Mountain

William Cullen Bryant, an American poet, wrote "Monument Mountain," a lyrical poem that tells the story of a Mohegan maiden whose forbidden love for her cousin caused her to leap from the mountain's cliffs. ...

There is a tale about these reverend rocks,
A sad tradition of unhappy love,
And sorrows borne and ended, long ago,
When over these fair vales the savage sought
His game in the thick woods. There was a maid,
The fairest of the Indian maids, bright-eyed,
With wealth of raven tresses, a light form,
And a gay heart. About her cabin-door
The wide old woods resounded with her song
And fairy laughter all the summer day.
She loved her cousin; such a love was deemed,
By the morality of those stern tribes,
Incestuous, and she struggled hard and long
Against her love, and reasoned with her heart,
As simple Indian maiden might.

William Cullen Bryant

Thousands climb the 1,735-foot Monument Mountain each year to enjoy the panoramic views of oak and pine forests interspersed with mountain laurel and birch. For almost two centuries, Monument Mountain has been a source of inspiration to poets like Bryant, novelists, and painters.

One legend says a Stockbridge Indian girl married a brave from another tribe, breaking tribal code. Her tribe condemned her, as many another had been condemned, to jump or to be thrown from the mountaintop. She refused to jump, so some of her tribesmen bound her hands and feet and carried her to the peak of the mountain. At dawn, as the tribe waited on the plain below, they threw the screaming girl off the cliff. But her kicking, screaming body did not clear a gnarled pine that grew from a crevice in the rocky side of the mountain. Instead, she dangled from one of its sturdy branches over the steep rocky ravine. She struggled to release herself from her bonds, trying to find an escape from her awful death on the rocks below, but without success. Sometimes, she cried out, and sometimes she just hung there, swaying on the branch. Those who had been waiting to see her die began to believe that they had condemned her unjustly.

A low-lying fog turned everything gray. The mountain brooded in the soft mist. The grim-faced braves of the tribe gathered around the council fire to decide what their next steps would be. Obviously, the spirits had disagreed with the sentence imposed on the girl. Some held that the punishment was fixed and nothing could alter it. Others felt that it still could be changed. As they argued, the heavens answered them.

Thunderclouds blanketed the skies. Lightning flashed and thunder echoed up and down the valley. As the Indians watched to see what would happen, a ball of fire descended through the clouds, enveloping both the tree and the girl. The flames paused for an instant. Then, flickering hard, they rose upward, cradling the beautiful Indian maiden in their hot sling. Higher and higher, this strange divine hammock rose, until it disappeared into the thunderheads.

People say that no Indian travels through the Monument Mountain pass without making a peace offering to the spirits who had saved the Indian girl from death on the rocks at the base of the peak. They cast a stone to the side of the path as they pray. Some believe that the rock cairn, which marks the spot where she lay buried, gives the mountain its name — Mountain of the Monument.

DIRECTIONS: From intersection of Routes 7 and 102 in Stockbridge Center, take Route 7 south and follow for three miles. Entrance and parking are on the right. From Great Barrington, take Route 7 north and follow for four miles to entrance on left.

Wahconah of Wahconah Falls

The pleasant valley of Dalton, in the Berkshire Hills, is near Wahconah Falls, which flows over several smaller tiered falls and then cascades into a deep pool. People who know how to listen to waterfalls say that sometimes these falls murmur happily because the wicked have been outwitted. At other times, they roar with laughter.

Chief Miacomo had ruled for forty years when Yonnongah, an aging Mohawk warlord, came to woo his beautiful daughter Wahconah. Yonnongah had three wives already, but he was determined to add Wahconah to his collection.

One June day, the girl sat beside the cascade named for her, braiding flowers in her hair and watching leaves float down the stream. Suddenly, she sensed that someone was watching her. She leapt to her feet in alarm as Nessacus, a handsome young brave, stepped forward, exclaiming, "Hail, Bright Star!"

"Hail, brother," answered Wahconah.

"I am Nessacus," said the man. "One of King Philip's soldiers.

My people and I are tired from our flight from the Long Knives (the English). Can we rest in your village?"

The maiden answered, "My father is absent. He is in council with the Mohawks, but his wigwams are always open. Please come with me."

Nessacus signaled to his tired, battle-worn troops. Wahconah led them down to her valley, where they were welcomed. As Nessacus' people were getting acquainted with Wahconah's tribe, the two young people found much to occupy their time. Over the next several weeks, they wandered the fields carpeted in the green and gold of fresh grass, walked along the upper portion of the falls, and swam under the falls. Soon, they were very much in love.

When her father Miacomo returned, he brought with him the elderly Mohawk suitor and the scheming priest, Tashmu, whom no one liked. During the next several weeks, the Indians played many games of skill and strength and had several great feasts. The youthful Nessacus easily won the games of skill, while the battle-scarred warrior Yonnongah won the games of strength. Nessacus quietly studied his opponent the way he analyzed his hunting grounds. After all, he was a hunter and to catch his prey he had to understand the universe in which he lived, the values that he had, and the methods that he used.

When Nessacus asked Wahconah's father permission to marry his daughter, Chief Miacomo was most pleased until Tashmu, the devious priest, intervened, advising him to give the girl to Yonnongah. A friendship with Yonnongah's tribe might be beneficial, given the expansion of the English, he said. Such a marriage would cement the bonds between the tribes, he declared. Miacomo felt harassed and frustrated.

The situation was at an impasse until Nessacus suggested that Yonnongah and he hold a duel; the winner would marry Wahconah. Yonnongah accepted this challenge, but the crafty Tashmu pointed to the negative omens in the voices of wind and thunder, the flight of birds, and shape of clouds. No good would come of such a duel, he warned. There would be problems. The Chief should let the Great Spirit meet with his wise and wily priest Tashmu instead.

"Go," snapped Chief Miacomo. "Commune with the wind and stars at Wizard's Glen. Let them tell us what to do."

Tashmu forbid anyone to leave the Indian village while he was conferring with the wind and the stars. When it was dark, he went to the pool below the falls instead of going to Wizard's Glen. Midway on the downstream side of the pool, he laid a great rock, dividing the current just about evenly. Working late into the night, he submerged many large rocks in the stream on one side, which diverted a greater share of water into the other.

In the morning, Tashmu announced that the Great Spirit had decreed that a canoe should be floated into the middle of the pool and left to drift. If it passed downstream on one side of the big rock, Nessacus was to have the girl. If it went to the other side, the great warrior Yonnongah would win. The assembled tribe listened eagerly for they wanted the lovely Wahconah to marry the young Nessacus.

Everything was prepared. The whole tribe gathered on the shores of the stream: Nessacus was on one side and Yonnongah on another. Tashmu set free the canoe; slowly, very slowly, it drifted toward the great stone. As it approached, it gained speed, veering one way and then the other. A shifting wind turned it sideways, and it struck the dividing rock amidships.

The tribe groaned. Then the current swung it around, a gust of wind caught it, and it swept past Nessacus — the winner! The tribe erupted in cheers of approval.

"The Great Spirit has spoken, and it is good," said Chief Miacomo. Dismayed, Tashmu and Yonnongah disappeared soon afterward, but not before Tashmu discovered that all the big rocks he had so carefully sunk on Nessacus' side of the brook weren't there. Someone had tricked him, and he knew who it was.

As the wedding festivities were progressing, a messenger brought word that the Long Knives were planning to destroy Chief Miacomo's tribe. Nessacus took Wahconah by the hand, promising to lead the tribe and her to a new home via the western trail.

DIRECTIONS: From Mass Pike I-90, take Exit 2 in Lee. Follow Route 20 west to Route 7 north for eleven miles to downtown Pittsfield. At Park Square rotary follow East Street for 3.25 miles (East Street becomes Merrill Road after 1.5 miles) to an intersection with Mass Route 9 east, and keep right. Turn right onto Route 9 east and follow for 4.6 miles through downtown Dalton to intersection with Mass Route 8A. Turn left and continue to follow Route 9 east /Route 8A north/North Street for 2.6 miles to North Street/Wahconah Falls Road. Look for brown lead-in signs. Turn right and follow for 0.5 mile (becomes unpaved) to park entrance on the right.

The fogs can lie low against the land.

Part Two:

Legends of the Berkshires

The Native American population of Stockbridge supported the English colonists during the French and Indian War. Along with the Mohawk tribe, they sided with the Patriots during the Revolution. One company served with the famed Rogers Rangers in 1756, and another fought with George Washington at White Plains twenty years later. Sadly, despite their loyalty, they were forced to move west after the Revolution, eventually settling in Wisconsin and Oklahoma, where their descendants are today.

The Berkshires played a major role during the American Revolution. Many conflicts took place between the Patriots and their neighbors with Royalist sympathies. At the Berkshire Congress in 1774, local delegates signed a document declaring the principles of separation from Britain, and Lenox residents endorsed a boycott of British goods. In 1776, militia from Berkshire County participated in the taking of Fort Ticonderoga and fought at White Plains in 1776 and, later, at Bennington during Burgoyne's advance from Canada in 1777.

Many legends of lingering specters from this period abound in the area.

Berkshire Tories and Patriots

Think of hot tar, a naked body, feathers, and an angry mob.

Patriots often tarred and feathered "obnoxious Tories" or Loyalists, terms used to describe those who remained loyal to the British Crown during the American Revolution. Once they poured hot tar over the Tory, they rolled him in feathers and paraded the goose-down victim about the streets in a cart to the enjoyment of the crowd.

Some Tories were forced to ride the rail, which involved placing the unhappy victim upon sharp rails with one leg on each side. Each rail was carried upon the shoulders of two tall men, with a man on each side to keep the poor wretch straight and fixed in his seat.

As the revolution progressed, semi-official organizations began to harass the Tories. Early in 1776, the Continental Congress suggested that Tories be disarmed; the local committees in the colonies then implemented the recommendation. Tories were arrested, tried, exiled to other districts and, in some cases, imprisoned.

Once the Second Continental Congress adopted the Declaration of Independence on July 4, 1776, declaring that the thirteen colonies were independent of Great Britain, loyalty to the British Crown became the equivalent of treason. All colonists were required to swear allegiance to their state of residence. Those who took the oath were issued a certificate of safety from arrest. Failure to take the oath meant possible imprisonment, confiscation of property, and even death.

In general, the oath prescribed loyalty to the Patriot cause, disloyalty to the British government, and a promise not to aid and abet the enemy. The Tory who refused to take the oath of allegiance became an outlaw. Life was a great deal easier if he became a Patriot.

But some didn't...

The Old Curmudgeon

One Tory in Lenox aggravated his neighbors by criticizing everything American — from the Governor on down. And, though this old Tory was a well-respected member of the gentry, the neighbors could no longer endure his abuse. A committee informed him that he could either swear allegiance to the colonies or be hanged. He declared, "I'd rather be hanged than swear allegiance to THOSE people."

So hanged he was on a ready-made gallow in the street. The Patriots let him down after a few minutes, revived him with rum, and offered the oath again.

"Absolutely not," he snarled.

The committee members were troubled. They had assumed that he would forego his loyalty to George III once the cord was put around his neck. After some debate, they hoisted him up again on the gallows. One committee member yanked the noose to show they meant business.

The old curmudgeon hung for some time. When lowered, he gave no sign of life. The committee members were horrified. They didn't want to kill the old fellow; they just wanted him to swear fealty to the American government. They worked hard to bring him back. At last, his lungs heaved, the purple faded from his cheeks, his eyes opened, and he gasped, "I'll swear."

The committee members cheered. Hurrying him to the tavern, they seated the former Tory before the fire, and put a glass of punch in his hand. After drinking to George Washington's health, he muttered, "It's a hard way to make Whigs, but it'll do."

The Honest Tory

Nathan Jackson, of Tyringham, was another Tory who had taken arms against his friends and neighbors. When captured, he was charged with treason and sent to jail to await trial. Now people in those days were so law abiding that the Great Barrington jail was rarely used. Although Jackson could easily have walked out of this flimsy jail, he believed that if he fled he would have been admitting to the injustice of Tory principles — and he was known to be an honest man.

He found life in jail so monotonous, however, that he asked the sheriff to let him work during the day, promising to sleep in his cell. The sheriff granted his request, given Jackson's reputation for honesty. Every night Jackson dutifully returned to jail.

It was harvesting time when the court planned to meet in Springfield. Harvesting time was not a good time for the sheriff to journey fifty miles to Springfield. Besides, he only had one case: Jackson. The sheriff was much relieved when Jackson pointed out, "I am a honest man. I can go alone."

So Jackson began the long trek to Springfield, where he would be tried for treason. On the way, he met Mr. Edwards of the Executive Council. Without telling his own name or office, Mr. Edwards learned the unusual reason that this lonely traveler was walking to Springfield.

When Jackson arrived, he was tried; he admitted to the charges against him and was sentenced to death. As he waited in jail, the Executive Council in Boston reviewed the cases. Mr. Edwards asked if there were any petitions for clemency in favor of Nathan Jackson. There weren't. Then, Mr. Edwards related the circumstance of his meeting with the condemned man on the lonely road to Springfield. The council members expressed their surprise and admiration for the honest Jackson. They sent a dispatch to Springfield countermanding the court findings. The prison door was flung open. Jackson was free.

The Tories' Cave

Supposedly, "Wheatleigh," which overlooks Lily Pond in Stockbridge, was the farm of Gideon Smith, a determined Tory. To avoid punishment, he hid from Berkshire Patriots during the War for Independence in a cave, which has since acquired the name Tories' Glen. The cave is at the base of October Mountain, close to Roaring Brook in what is known as New Lenox.

Gideon hid in the two small rooms of the cave for weeks. The Indians supplied him with food and his wife walked their children daily before the cave opening so he could see their faces. In May 1776, he harbored Captain McKay, a British prisoner of war, who had escaped from Hartford. Once the townspeople learned he had provided a safe spot to the enemy, they were irate.

They took Linus Parker, a famous Lenox sharp shooter and Gideon's friend, to his house. There, they found him hiding in his barn.

The story does not say what happened to Gideon at this point. It does say that Gideon and Linus resumed their friendship after the war.

One day Gideon asked Linus, "I want to know if you really would have shot me?"

"As quick as I ever shot a deer," Linus replied.

Subsequently, the cave has provided safe harbor to a pair of bobcats and a teenage couple, whose parents disapproved of their romance. They lived there for several days while everyone sought them. Ironically, the girl married another man.

(Note: Charles Sheldon French has written a poem about this incident, called "The Tories Cave, Lenox." Perry, p. 133-135.)

DIRECTIONS: An enchanting road to Tory Glen winds through New Lenox past the Gothic St. Helena Chapel, set in this lovely spot at the foot of Washington Mountain by the Hon. John E. Parsons in memory of his daughter.

The Case of the Phantom Soldiers

In the first decade of independence, the Berkshires witnessed Shay's Rebellion, which occurred when former Continental soldiers revolted against the ways the new federal government was disrupting local economics and autonomy. Colonel Ashley (see Mum Bett, p. 175) and local militia engaged a band of rebels along what is now Egremont Road in Sheffield, Massachusetts, killing several and wounding more than thirty.

Caleb Hudson was a scoundrel. A deserter, a looter, and a Tory, he was just looking for trouble. And he got it…

The story goes that he deserted from the Continental Army after the Battle of Breed's Hill in Charlestown, Massachusetts. Although he was a Tory, he didn't want to do anything that might compromise him and his position in the Berkshires. So he became a local nuisance and a small-time looter of Patriots' homes.

The local Tories decided that they should be the ones to kidnap General Washington. It would be a great feather in their caps. Many attempts had been made, but none were successful.

Their spies told them that General Washington was planning to meet with the colonial troops based in Connecticut and eastern New York, which was where Washington intended to stop the advance of British troops under General Tyron. The Tories decided they could slip into the colonial camp and kidnap Washington. They selected six men to carry out this task. Much to his consternation, Caleb Hudson was one of them.

Each of the six men would ride south separately. Once there, they would assemble in Ridgefield, Connecticut, near Washington's headquarters.

Our reluctant crook began riding south. Just before crossing the Housatonic River in south Lee, he heard the distinctive, tromping rhythm of marching feet. It sounded like hundreds of feet! Then he saw the flags and an entire regiment of continental soldiers. There were hundreds…maybe thousands!

Afraid that he would be recognized as a deserter or forced into the Army again, he hid in the underbrush on the edge of the path. Columns of soldiers tromped by, eight abreast. These colorless, zombie-like soldiers weren't making any noise. There wasn't any talk, any beating of drums, or blowing of fifes. No equipment rattled, no wagons creaked, no sound was made — other than the tromping of their boots.

Sensing the unworldly, his mare became upset. Caleb could not keep her quiet, but the robot soldiers never noticed. They just marched to the river's edge. Then all those ranks of soldiers proceeded into the river in perfect cadence. Not a single soldier came out on the other side. They simply vanished.

At this point, Caleb's horse panicked and galloped away. Terrified, he clung to the saddle. He did not stop or slow down until he reached South Lee Inn, where he downed several glasses of flip and told the bartender about the spectral soldiers. From then on, Caleb Hudson never dabbled in the Tory cause again.

The Undead Hessian

During the American War for Independence, George III made a deal with Fredrick II and hired Hessian mercenaries from Hesse-Kassel (the land of Grimm's fairy tales) to fight for the British. The British often hired Germans and other nationalities to do their fighting. During the Revolution, Hessians generally remained in their own units with their own officers.

Hessian soldier, Franz Wagner, an exception to the rule, was attached to General Burgoyne's forces. Wounded at the Battle of Saratoga, he died while making his way south. Some North Egremont men buried him in the local burial ground, but, unfortunately, he refused to remain dead. His energy or soul had become caught between this plane of existence and the next.

People in the area began to see him wandering about at night. One even saw him in his full green Hessian uniform wandering around the cemetery; another saw him wandering along the banks of the Green River. Children giggled about the bogeyman or the specter. Women talked quietly at church. Men worried.

As the stories about the specter of the Hessian soldier multiplied, some of the village elders decided to verify the rumors by going out one night to the burial ground. Joe Tanner and Tom Hendricks, who were the most adventuresome, went ahead while the rest of the group followed — very reluctantly. They walked to the Hessian's grass-covered grave, but nothing was there. Just as they began to feel silly and wondered what their wives would say, a specter loomed over them. Several men jumped and ran, terrified. Their hearts pounding, Joe and Tom stood near the grave. The specter came closer. They thought he was trying to speak from his fearsome grimaces, but they heard no words. The closer the specter came, the more frightened they became. Finally, the grimacing specter was too much for them, and they too turned and ran.

Joe felt very foolish when he returned home. It was just a specter after all. It wasn't real – not really.

The beauty of the Berkshires is well known.

Meanwhile, as news of their encounter made its way around town, the unease in Egremont increased to a state of terror. People stopped going out after sunset. Not even a church meeting or prayer group could get them to venture forth. When they came home after work, they bolted their doors. They draped their windows. They kept fires lit in the fireplace should the specter decide to come in through the chimney.

Finally, Joe Tanner announced, "Enough. We need to put this specter to rest." He convened a group of the bolder villagers to discuss the matter. After an intense discussion, Tanner suggested that perhaps, if they moved the Hessian's grave to some other location, the specter would move on and leave them alone. Some men were concerned that they might get in trouble with the authorities; many were uncertain about disinterring a corpse. Someone wondered out loud whether the Hessian was still alive. By the meeting's end, however, no one else had offered a better plan so they began to prepare.

On the appointed night, the men assembled on horseback. Tanner brought his wagon for transporting the casket. Sentries were posted at both sides of the burial ground just in case someone came along. Those men who had volunteered to dig began the gruesome task of disinterring the Hessian. The first few feet of dirt was frozen solid, and it broke up in chunks with the smaller pieces sharp as glass. Eventually, their shovels hit the coffin's edge. They slid the wooden box out carefully. Presumably, the coffin was filled with Wagner's specter and his remains. Feeling very pleased that the hardest part of their self-imposed task was completed, the group headed northeast in the darkness. Joe Tanner and two others rode in the wagon with the Hessian. The rest of the men were on horseback. When they reached the eastern side of Tom Ball Mountain, they found the road too treacherous for the wagon. So Tanner and the other two men left the others with the coffin, and they went ahead into the forest to locate a burial spot.

They hadn't gone very far when they heard men screaming. Running back to the wagon, they saw the specter sitting on top of his coffin. Once again, he was making ugly grimaces, but no sound came out. The men who had been guarding him had run away from the wagon. They hid behind trees and rocks, afraid that the specter would hurt them. As Tanner shamed the men into coming back, the specter slipped away.

The men grabbed the coffin and headed into the woods. They went partially up the eastern base of the mountain to a natural hollow. There, they grabbed their spades and began digging as fast as they could. When they had dug a suitable hole, they lowered the coffin inside carefully — they didn't want to enrage the Hessian more than necessary. They covered the new grave with dirt and leaves and rode away as fast as they could.

They did not speak of the incident again until many weeks later when they heard that Stockbridge citizens were saying that they had seen a Hessian soldier wandering the woods around West Stockbridge. Much to Joe Tanner's delight, the Hessian never appeared in Egremont again.

To Counterfeit Is Death

Many of us have looked for buried treasure sometime during our lives. I always wondered about hidden drawers in desks and holes in old trees (Nancy Drew was always finding things there); others dive

around shipwrecks; and some still think treasures can be discovered in

the granite caves found throughout the Berkshires.

One of the Berkshire's more quaintly named geological features is Bung Hill, a 25-foot-high bump on the gentle surrounding landscape in Great Barrington, Massachusetts. Major William King, Jr., a veteran of the French and Indian wars, named it Bung Hill because of its resemblance to a keg bung or stopper. Snakes and other animals laze in the sun on the bump's granite surfaces.

Halfway up the hill in the rocky northeastern face is a broad opening into the hillside marked by an overhanging sharp blade of stone. The passage soon narrows. A stack of fragmented fallen rocks forms a three-foot or so barrier to a chamber about thirty feet long and eight to ten feet wide. A solid block of stone more than fifty feet long acts as the ceiling and the eastern wall. Two small apertures light this inner room; the blackened walls around one opening testify to its use as a chimney.

In 1765, Gill Belcher, a silversmith, moved from Hebron, Connecticut, to Great Barrington, where he bought "Bung Hill." On the northern side of the hill stood a small house. There, Belcher settled himself and began working in silver and gold. Not much is known about him from that time, but eight years later, he said he was a family man with nine small children; the eldest was just twelve. He also said he was the only son of an aged mother. Perhaps that is why he turned to making money!

Now, in the pre-revolutionary days, the United States did not have a universal monetary system. Instead, the different colonies established their own system. The Province of New York, for example, had its own official imprint and coin. Its notes were emblazoned with "To Counterfeit Is Death." Unfortunately, threats don't always stop the would-be criminal.

Gil Belcher and some associates began counterfeiting silver coins and notes in the Bung Hill cave. Militiamen caught them in the act of manufacturing counterfeit "York money." Supposedly, the damning clue in finding the counterfeiters was smoke issuing from the crevices of the rocks of the cave.

At the same time, other counterfeiters were arrested through New England. According to the *Hartford Courant* (Dec. 1, 1772), twelve men were placed in custody in Albany. One of these said that extensive counterfeiting had been occurring on the Massachusetts/New York border.

In December 1772, Belcher and two of his associates, John Wall Lovely and Dr. Joseph Bill, tried to escape, but their attempt was frustrated. The three of them were condemned to death by hanging on April 2, 1773.

On January 5, 1773, Gill Belcher petitioned New York Governor Tryon for a pardon. He said, "Humbly prays your Excellency to take peity (sic) on a poor helpless Mortal who has no friends but a poor helpless family of a wife and Nine Small Children…." (Perry, p. 40). The New York state archives still have this document marked with "Not acted upon." Belcher then appealed to the Massachusetts Legislature, pointing out that if he did commit the crime it occurred in Massachusetts and not in New York. Therefore, Massachusetts should be responsible for him. But Massachusetts ignored him.

On April 1, the three condemned men managed to free themselves from their chains and nearly escaped, but they were discovered and confined again. By morning, they had freed themselves from their chains again and barricaded the room in which they were imprisoned. They swore to kill anyone who attempted to remove them.

The authorities sent out a general alarm. They put the militia under arms. Most of the general population was armed too, given the situation. The prisoners set fire to the jail, but the flames were extinguished. Lovely threatened to blow up several pounds of gunpowder that he had procured. Finally, the militia broke in and, after a struggle, carried them to the gallows, where they were hung.

The Hartford Courant (April 13, 1773) published Belcher's last speech, confession and dying words. In it, he said, "I met with people (who) was perversely inclined as myself; we soon became associated and concerted schemes which had no tendency to promote the interest of our neighbors. No gain afforded so much pleasure as that which I acquired by illicit means. Coining and counterfeiting engrossed my attention, and those who first advised me to transgress, persuaded me to continue my iniquitous practices."

DIRECTIONS: The cave is high in the steep slopes of the Roaring Brook ravine in Great Barrington.

'Tis the Gift to Be Simple

The Shakers, or United Society of Believers in Christ's Second Appearing, are one of the most successful communal societies established in America in the late Eighteenth and early Nineteenth centuries. Their founder, Mother Ann Lee, an English mill worker, emigrated from Manchester, England in 1774. She and other early Shakers established communities connected by their shared faith and a commitment to celibacy, common property, gender equality, pacifism, and separation from the world. They were committed to creating heaven on earth.

By the 1860s, some 6,000 Shakers were living in eighteen communities in New England, New York, Ohio, Kentucky, and Indiana. Today, the sect is virtually extinct, since Mother Ann regarded sex as a device of the devil, and Shaker "brothers" and "sisters" lived in separate dormitories. Their only mutual recreation was prayer meetings, at which they sang hymns and "shook" together in frenzied dances. Their shaking and trembling at their worship services was the way they rid themselves of evil...hence the name.

Mother Ann Lee admonished her followers to "put your hands to work and your hearts to God." The results can be seen in their craftsmanship, which is world renown for its elegant simplicity. Credited with a multitude of innovations, they invented a flat broom, an apple parer, a circular saw and many other labor-saving devices, based on their belief in simplicity, purity and perfection. Even today, architects and designers attempt to replicate their spare yet elegant furniture and utensils.

Well known for their medicinal herb and garden seed industries, Shaker communities cultivated herbs, raised produce for seed, and processed herbs and plants (e.g., belladonna, hops, native ginger, chicory, dandelions, wormseed, black cohosh, basil, poppies, and pennyroyal) for sale to the "World." Supposedly, seed packets began with them!

The Hancock Shaker Village in Pittsfield, Massachusetts is a popular tourist attraction in the Berkshires. Visitors have the unique opportunity of going back in time by a century or two and touring this graceful, renovated village with its twelve hundred acres of farm, woodland, and pasture. Heritage breeds of animals such as shorthorn cattle, Merino sheep, and silver-laced Wyandotte and Dominique chickens roam the fields. Two heirloom vegetable gardens contain plant varieties on Shaker seed lists from the 1830s and 1890s, respectively.

The buildings hold a major collection of Shaker furniture and household items. "Wherever you go, you feel that you are beyond the realm of hurry," wrote one visitor in 1977. "There is no restlessness, or fret of business, or anxiety; it is as if the work was done, and it was one eternal afternoon." (Time Magazine, 1969)

But like most villages... this one has its own story.

Every Shaker society has a place for meeting in the open air, usually at some little distance from their village. There they assemble at least twice in the year. Usually, on these hills there is a building with two apartments: one for the sisters; the other, for the brothers. A fountain acts as the center for their marches, dances, songs, and plays.

Mount Sinai, named for the mountain where Moses laid down the Ten Commandments for the Israelites, is on the grounds of Hancock Shaker Village. This Berkshire landmark is a sacred hill to the community.

As the story goes, the Hancock Shaker community was living under the threat of eternal hellfire. As their elders told them, the Lord had raised their foes high against them. Sisters in other communities, who had been known for their staunch devoutness, had become covered in darkness and lust, eloping with corrupt freethinkers. Brothers were not abstaining from lust and uncleanness but enjoying card games and carnal pleasures. Obviously, it was difficult to be celibate and devoted to the Shaker virtues of simplicity, purity and perfection, when the rest of the world chose to remain in a state of corruption. The adherents of the antichristian teachers had broken the laws, disobeyed the statutes, and violated the eternal covenant in their folly and blindness. Surely, Sodom and Gomorrah never went so deep in sin. The world had become a frightening place.

Their Elder Gabriel Patton was most distressed about these evil influences on his flock. With eyes burning, he exhorted them to be aware of the Devil's influence. "This powerful, unseen evil spirit is a master of lies and deception. He has blinded you to God's truth. Satan has dominated people from the time of Adam and Eve. We want what we shouldn't have; we long for sinful things. If you unlock that door so temptation can get in, you are sinning. Let God in instead. Come to Zion and wander no more."

One member of the community was Sister Martha Tomlinson, a young woman whose husband and child had died. She came from the eastern part of the state. Initially, she had seemed quite content with her decision to accept the Shaker way of life. During the past several months, however, she had been deeply depressed, often weeping throughout the night. Several of the sisters were concerned that she no longer gave her superiors the customary reverence and showed the requisite obedience to their ways. Consequently, they subjected her to a multitude of penances, such as compelling her not only to kneel, but also to prostrate herself before Eldress Mary. Even that humiliation was without effect.

Elder Patton said, "Like John said, the whole world is under the control of the evil one. The world values those things that are contrary to God's will." Elder Patton was afraid that his people would succumb to the worldly ways of the unbelievers.

He cautioned, "The Devil has successfully turned other sisters and brothers away from God. Be careful, my brothers and sisters. He is trying to tempt you. The Devil is all around us. Satan is attacking our community, and his demons are fighting to control, influence, entice, and dominate us. They devise cunning schemes against us and conspire to make us weak. Be strong."

Believing that Satan and his forces were assembling at Mount Sinai, he told the assembled community that Sinai was where the true believers would defeat the Devil. "Prepare ye, my sisters and brothers, for the final battle. With the help of the Lord, we shall strike down the evil one."

On the appointed day for the battle, every able-bodied brother and sister in the Shaker community assembled. Only Sister Tomlinson, who was in bed with a fever, was absent.

In the early dawn, they gathered in the meetinghouse, where the elders stood at one end of the hall, and the eldresses at the other end. Two brothers approached together and knelt down before the elders, and two sisters approached the eldresses. The elders and eldresses pantomimed throwing something towards the kneeling brothers and sisters. It is said that two little angels standing close by received the suits of invisible armor from the elders and clothed the faithful subjects in these suits, which had the power to shield the truly faithful from the Devil. And so the Shakers, who were pacifists in the temporal world, were clothed with the glorious apparel of righteousness. In this way, they prepared to battle the Devil, the Power of Darkness.

In the early dawn, the faithful Shakers formed a ring around the base of Mt. Sinai and began to ascend the mountain. Dressed in invisible armor, each one carried a Bible in one hand and the sword of the Spirit in the other. Singing one of their early ballad hymns, "Mother," they marched shoulder-to-shoulder, finding pleasure in their strength and unity.

At the top of the mount, they began to narrow the circle around the Devil. As they drew their circle tighter and tighter, a vile odor filled the air. The Shakers recognized the stench: they knew it was the smell of sulfur and brimstone. When their ring became so tight that they could see their reflection in each other's eyes, they heard the sounds of the Devil: horrendous howls, harsh curses, and the sibilant preternatural hissing of that serpent of evil. Elder Patton commanded them to advance still further, so that the Devil would be prevented from escaping. With a bestial shriek, the Devil died.

Hancock Shaker Village is nestled on 1,200 acres of farm, woodland, and meadow.

The Shakers celebrated their formidable victory with fervent singing, dancing, whirling, and shaking. The young sisters turned so swiftly that the air gathering under their skirts raised them, exposing their red petticoats and other underclothes. Sometimes in their enthusiasm one or two would fall prostrate upon the floor.

Later they found that the Devil's final victim was Martha Tomlinson, who had ended her life.

DIRECTIONS: Hancock Shaker Village is located on Route 20 in Pittsfield, Massachusetts, just west of the junction of Routes 20 and 41. Known as "The City of Peace," the village contains the largest and most representative collection of Shaker artifacts available to the public at an original Shaker site. Its furniture, tools and equipment, household objects, textiles, manuscripts, and inspirational art reflect the Shakers' role in the life of America.

Phantom Locomotive

Ghosts on trains, planes and automobiles are often found.

Some Pittsfield, Massachusetts residents are convinced that a ghost train comes and goes on a stretch of track between the North Street bridge and the junction.

One afternoon in February 1958, owner John Quirk and several of his customers in the Bridge Lunch Diner saw a ghost train come and go through town. Although everyone tried to convince them they had seen something else, Quirk told reporters and railroad officials that they had seen a ghostly steam locomotive with a coal tender. It pulled five coaches and a baggage car. Their view was so clear that they could even see the coal in the tender. They did not see any workman at the throttle or stoking the engine, however.

The railroad officials didn't believe him. They said their description did not match any type of train in use. They said that there definitely hadn't been a train that passed Union Depot or the junction at that time.

Then one cold March morning, the Bridge Lunch Diner employees and customers saw the ghost train again. According to the waiter, every customer saw the train—and, just like before, the steam engine pulled a baggage car, five coaches and was heading east towards Boston.

All aboard, the phantom express!

Berkshire's Bigfoot

For years, scientists and researchers have speculated about and searched for an enigmatic creature known as Bigfoot. Legendary in the annals of American folklore, Bigfoot is a large ape-like creature reportedly sighted hundreds of times in the United States and Canada (most often in the Pacific Northwest) since the mid-nineteenth century. Similar to the Loch Ness monster and the Abominable Snowman, Bigfoot is variously described as standing seven to ten feet tall and weighing over five hundred pounds with footprints seventeen inches long. Sasquatch is a Native American name for the creature.

Most scientists discount the existence of Bigfoot, and some supposed footprints of the animal are known to be hoaxes, but the Bigfoot Field Researchers Organization (BFRO) reports many sightings. And, we are in the Berkshires … where strange things happen.

In fact, the October 18, 1879 edition of the *New York Times* reported that two young Vermont men hunting in the mountains south of Williamstown saw a "Creature being about five feet high, resembling a man in form and movement, but covered all over with bright red hair, and having a long straggling beard and with very wild eyes. When first seen, the creature sprang from behind a rocky cliff and started for the woods nearby. Although terrified, one of the men fired at the creature. He assumed that he wounded it, for with fierce cries of pain and rage, it turned on its assailants, who fled at the highest speed possible. Although they lost their guns and ammunition in their flight, they dared not return for fear of encountering this horrifying being."

And, on August 23, 1983, according to *The Berkshire Eagle*, picnickers reported seeing a weird mountain "creature."

"It stood on two legs, silhouetted on the trail in the moonlight, and it was huge. I don't scare easily, but it scared me." So said Eric Durant, 18, one of two men who came to the Eagle office yesterday to report their sighting of a strange humanlike 'creature' Sunday night on October Mountain." He and his companion Frederick Parody, 22, said the episode took place near the former Boy Scout Camp Eagle, which is on Felton Lake in the town of Washington and has been abandoned since 1970. They said they had been having a steak and chicken cookout with two friends when they heard noises in the woods. Around midnight, he and one of the others decided to investigate. When they were about one hundred yards away from the cookout site, they spotted the creature fifty yards ahead of them on the trail, silhouetted in the moonlight.

As the quartet was about to leave, the headlights of their car shone on the creature, lurking behind some bushes, according to Durant and Parody. They said it was erected on two legs and was six to seven feet tall. It was dark brown in color and had strange eyes that glowed, they said. Both were emphatic in saying that it was not a bear. Parody said he has hunted bears in Maine and was quite familiar with how they look.

Of course, they ran, knowing that he must be right behind them as is often the case when we dream. The thing, whatever it is, is always right at our heels — and we can smell its fetid breath.

On Wednesday, August 26, 1998, a lone hiker traversing a well-used trail on October Mountain reported seeing a creature moving stones and small pieces of wood in the October Mountain State forest (Lenoxdale in BFRO, Report #1199).

"At first all I could see were arms moving and an occasional glimpse of a fur-covered body. At first I thought I was looking at a large black bear, which are not uncommon in the area. I pulled a pair of 40-power binoculars from my travel pack and attempted to focus on the object. Again it was difficult because of all the brush. At one point the animal moved into a slight clearing, it was then that I realized I was observing something very unusual!

"A very tall and slightly stooped animal with a massive body covered completely with reddish hair." The hiker added that the head was rather pointed and covered with hair or fur; the face was dark in color and had less hair than the top of the head and the neck seemed to be non-existent. After recovering from his fright, he noticed that it "was moving stones and small pieces of wood and grubbing for either roots or insects." When he got closer, he could see that "...it was not human. The arms were too long and the face seemed very distorted and elongated. The arms extended past the kneecaps!"

That was several years ago, but be careful when you go hiking by yourself in the Berkshires. You can't always tell what's lying in those deep-dappled shadows.

DIRECTIONS: October Mountain State Forest, 256 Woodland Road, Lee, Massachusetts. Follow U.S. Route 20 west for 1.1 miles through downtown Lee to Center Street. Turn right onto Center Street and follow (becomes Columbia Street) for one mile to Bradley Street. Turn right onto Bradley Street (becomes Woodland Road) and follow brown lead-in signs; it's one mile to the campground entrance.

Part Three

Lore of the Berkshires

The Berkshires were a formidable wilderness. For a long time, the Indians enjoyed their great valleys and lakes uninhibited. In the late 1600s, long after colonial society was established in eastern Massachusetts and the Hudson River Valley, some Dutch settlers moved into the territory. Initially, the Mohegans and the colonial settlers coexisted peacefully, but unfortunately, man's greed for land overcame that noble purpose, and the Indians were pushed out.

These stories are told from a fictional perspective, trying to make sense of the past. Those voices from previous generations must be heard—their stories must be told...

Balanced Rock

Massachusetts has many unusual stone structures of uncertain antiquity and unknown origin. Some have attributed them to ancient Celts, Native Americans, colonial farmers, and neo-pagans. During the ice age, a great glacier deposited Balance Rock, or Rolling Rock, near Pittsfield, Massachusetts.

This great block of stone weighs many tons, and is delicately balanced on a little rock beneath it. Many have tried to push it off, but it stands steady and strong. Along with trying to push it over, many people have told stories about Balanced Rock. One of the best is the following...

Near the rock, one of the Atotarhos, kings of the Six Nations, had his camp. He was a notorious and much feared warrior. The story says he ate and drank from bowls made of the skulls of enemies. He wrapped live poisonous snakes around his body when he held audiences. They crawled up his arms, tongues flickering. He terrified everyone, and all of the braves and the boys in the tribe idolized him. They all wanted to be as strong, as tough, as feared as he.

All but one that is — his youngest son. He was skinny, small, and liked to watch the river flow, the birds fly, the sunset slide into the lake. Sometimes he even picked flowers for his mother. His father was repelled by this behavior. How could he have such a weakling for a son!

One day, the chief's son stood near Balanced Rock watching a number of boys stack one rock upon another and then throw rocks in an effort to knock the just-built rock tower down.

Another boy said, "Bet you can't do it. Bet you can't."

Another one added, "Of course, he can't. He only stares at the water and watches the birds." The chief's son just stood silently watching.

"Sissy," said a third.

"What a coward," sneered a fourth. "You won't even try."

His father, who had been watching, turned away in disgust.

As the boy stepped forward, their malicious laughter changed to cries of astonishment and fear. Hearing the change in their voices, the chief turned back.

His son towered above them, a giant among mere mortals.

This giant picked up an enormous rock and tossed it from one giant hand to another as if it was a mere pebble. He went to the edge of the woods, picked up an enormous boulder and lifted it to its precarious stand on bedrock, where it stands balanced to this day.

He then stood back and laughed at the other boys, who stood with their mouths open wide. "Next time don't judge another brave so quickly," he declared.

DIRECTIONS: From Mass Pike, take Exit 2 and follow U.S. Route 20 west for eleven miles to downtown Pittsfield. Turn left at the light and continue on U.S. Route 20 west for 2.2 miles. Turn right onto Hungerford Avenue, continue for 0.2 miles, then bear left onto Fort Hill Avenue and continue for one mile. Turn left onto West Street. Continue for 0.2 miles, and turn right onto Churchill Street, and continue for 1.7 miles to Cascade Street. Turn left and follow the brown lead-in signs to the park. Balance Rock State Park is located in the northeast corner of Pittsfield State Forest.

"Hail to the Sunrise," a Mohawk Indian Memorial is located on Route 2 in Charlemont, Massachusetts.

The White Deer of Onata

In the early sixteenth century, the French had been encroaching on the British territory in America. Already, France claimed most of North America west of the Appalachian Mountains. Jacques Cartier (1542) and Samuel de Champlain (1608) had established military outposts along the St. Lawrence River and into the Great Lakes, founding the territory known as New France. Trappers, traders, and Jesuit missionaries, along with Indians, inhabited this wilderness.

They competed for the Indians' furs, suborned the native tribes, and searched for the path to the Pacific. They learned the Indian dialects, adopted their habits, and tried to convert them. Unlike the English, who took axes and saws to the wilderness, the French were adventurers – not farmers.

Because of the riches to be found in the New World, many young French nobles sailed to New France to find their fortune. To get ahead in the French Court, you had to please the king: Louis XV. All the courtiers knew that he loved presents: jewels, gold, furs.

During the early days of the French and Indian War, an ambitious French officer named Montalbert was sent to Berkshire County to persuade the Housatonic Indians to wage war against the English. Montalbert was not only an adventurer; he was an ambitious man. He wanted to climb the ranks of nobility.

The Housatonic Indians were a prosperous tribe living near to the deep, spring-fed Lake Onoto, which supplied them with fish and game. They attributed their good fortune to a white doe, which came to drink from the lake. Obviously, she was a good omen. One of their prophets had predicted, "So long as the white doe drinks at Onota, pestilence, famine and foe will never lay waste to their land."

The Housatonic Indians threatened anyone who tried to harm their white doe with swift retribution. They treated the doe so well that she allowed them to touch her, to pat her, even to play with her.

While Montalbert was visiting the village, he learned of the white doe. "What a treasure that would be!" he thought. "Such a unique curiosity! If it could bring happiness and prosperity to a small band of heathens, think what it could do for King Louis XV! And most certainly the king would reward his Montalbert accordingly. My fortune would be made, if I just brought the king the doe's skin."

The enterprising Montalbert immediately offered a great reward to the hunter who brought him the skin of the white deer. The Indians were appalled. The doe was sacred. Anyone who harmed it would quickly feel their vengeance. Recognizing this, Montalbert decided to find another way to obtain the doe.

In his meetings with the tribe, he noticed that one Indian named Wondo loved rum. He would do almost anything for a drink, and Montalbert, like other ambitious white men, had brought lots of rum for bribing susceptible Indians. Realizing that Wondo was the weak link, Montalbert plied him with rum.

Once Wondo had succumbed to the rum and no longer adhered to his tribe's values, Montalbert said he would give him a bottle of rum in exchange for the white doe. Rum was the most important thing in the world to Wondo — certainly more important than a white doe. So he brought the white doe to him. The doe came eagerly because she trusted people — even a drunken Indian didn't bother her. The Indians had always brought her joy and happiness, but the ambitious Montalbert wasn't an Indian — he killed the white doe with one quick blow. Placing her blood-splashed skin in his saddlebag, he left quickly for Canada.

Once Wondo finished his bottle of rum and realized that he had been manipulated, he felt awful. Not being able to live with his guilt, he confessed to his crime, and the tribe dealt with him swiftly. Then the tribe set out to stop Montalbert, hoping that they could prevent the approaching disaster.

The storytellers say that Montalbert never reached Canada, and that Louis XV never received the skin of the white deer. But the prosperity of the Indian tribe was no more. Wars, disease, emigration followed. In a few years not a wigwam was left standing besides Onoto.

The English Way of Life

In the late 1600s, long after colonial society was established in eastern Massachusetts and the Hudson River Valley, some Dutch settlers moved into the Berkshire territory. Initially, the Mohegans and the colonial settlers coexisted peacefully. In 1733, Sheffield was the first town to be incorporated in Berkshire County; Stockbridge was the second. It, however, is the only town whose purpose was to Christianize the natives and ensure that their land would be theirs forever.

A far-sighted Mohegan chef, Konkapot, recognized that he could not hope to defeat the white invaders who were busily establishing themselves as farmers on the lush virgin land of the Berkshires. Therefore, he decided if he couldn't fight them, he'd join them. His tribe would become Christian and learn to write and read English!

Konkapot observed: "There were ten Indians where there is now one. But the Christians greatly increase and multiply, and spread over the land; let us, therefore, leave our former courses and become Christians."

The sub-chief, Umpachene, was not so sure about embracing Christianity, but he did accompany Konkapot to Springfield in May 1734 to receive military ranks for having stood by the English in the ongoing French and Indian Wars (1689-1763). At that time, they also consulted with ministers of the established church – Puritan/Congregational – regarding the formation of a mission to the Indians along the Housatonic River.

Following negotiations, the Puritans responded by sending the young minister John Sergeant, a gentle, popular Yale tutor from Newark, New Jersey. He cheerfully agreed that he would give up the pleasures of life at Yale to work with the Indians. So for a very uncertain future and a small salary, the 24-year-old Sergeant accepted the offer from the Boston Commission on Indian Affairs to become the missionary pastor of the new Indian parish to be organized in the remote Berkshires. An agency of the London Society for the Propagation of the Gospel in New England, the Commission intended to create a mission among the Housatonic Indians in southern Berkshire County and to assist them in learning the English way of life.

Before making a firm decision, he journeyed to the valley and preached a sermon to Chief Konkapot and his family. He also converted an army-trained, English-speaking Indian named Poopoonah and baptized him as Ebenezer.

The Indians welcomed Sergeant happily. They built him a large wigwam for a meetinghouse and school, surrounding them with their wigwams. Their children went to the new school so to adjust to the English way of life. Sergeant appointed Timothy

Woodbridge as schoolmaster while he returned to New Haven to complete his own education. His companions were the chief's two sons, ages nine and eight, who accompanied him so they could learn each other's languages.

These two Indian boys must have been a rarity at Yale. Not only were they young, but they were also Indians being cared for by a young single man.

On July 5, 1735, the young earnest Yale graduate returned to work among the Indians. He was instantly successful, probably because of his immersion into their lives. He preached, baptized, and married people all that winter. When the Indians went into the woods the next February for their annual maple sugaring, Sergeant accompanied them so to continue prayer and instruction.

Ministering to and teaching two groups of Indians separated by some fifteen miles of dense wilderness and the steep slope of Monument Mountain taxed the physical resources of the two men. Realizing that by concentrating the Indians in one location, they could control the Indians more efficiently and open up more land for settlement, the colonial authorities arranged during the winter to consolidate the divided tribe on its land above the mountain at Wnahtukook. That land was to be reserved for the Indians forever. In 1736, the general court purchased from the Indians all the land at Skatehook and granted them the township now known as Stockbridge.

In their new village, the Indians were to be educated and converted; they would live in houses, cultivate farms, plant orchards, and learn typical English crafts. No longer would they be just hunters and gatherers, they would resemble the colonial farmers and lead settled, regulated colonial lives. Sergeant and Woodbridge were made owners of one-sixtieth part each, as were four white families who were recruited to provide role models of civilized English life. The tribe would hold the rest of the land in common as was the custom.

The colonial legislature appropriated money, and the Indians cleared more land for crops. In 1737 and 1738, the four white families built their homes on the hill (now Prospect Hill) rather than living in town. One of the newcomers, Ephraim Williams, Sergeant's future father-in-law, chose the hill because of its view and its distance from the natives. Incidentally, that part of town is still the area that includes the largest and finest houses. Only Timothy Woodbridge, with his bride and Sergeant, lived in a house among the Indians in Indian Town.

The Indians were determined to succeed in their new village and worked diligently. Using English methods, the Indians harvested more than three times their usual crops. Governor Belcher and interested groups and persons in London contributed funds. To enhance the success of the missionary enterprise, Indian Town was chartered in 1737 and incorporated in 1739 as the town of Stockbridge. From then on, its inhabitants were known as Stockbridge Indians.

Sergeant's vision of incorporating the colonial way of life with the Indian culture appeared to have been achieved. Even the elective offices of the new town were shared among the colonials and the Indians.

That same year, the saintly Sergeant married high-spirited Abigail Williams, daughter of Ephraim Williams, one of the white settlers. The house he built her, preserved today as a museum called Mission House, was quite grand for the time. The paneled doorway with its elaborate woodworking was carved in Connecticut and dragged by oxen over fifty miles of rugged terrain. She maintained the household and raised their children, and he concentrated on converting the Indians and turning them into "civil, industrious and polished people."

Over the years, the Indians built English houses along a 'street' running east and west through the center of town. The trees were cleared, and the church at one end of town was surrounded by the town green and bordered by the graveyard. Then Konkapot and the Sergeant died. With Sergeant's death, the Indians lost their champion, and the terms of their settlement were increasingly violated.

Although the Indians and the English were supposed to be equal, the ever-increasing colonial population and their influence overwhelmed the Indians. Unscrupulous whites began to seize land that was promised to the Indians in perpetuity. Among them was Sergeant's father-in-law. The Dutch traders supplied the Indians with alcohol and endeavored to convince them that the English were enslaving them.

General Joseph Dwight, who was appointed to manage the town, married Abigail Sergeant. Under the influence of her father, Ephraim Williams, he became involved in selling liquor to the Indians and the mismanagement of the Mission School. The Indians became so dispirited that the school "mysteriously" burned down.

Ultimately, the largely landless Indians left Stockbridge in 1785. After being displaced several times by the relentless pressure of the white settlers' westward migration, they settled, in 1850, on a reservation near Shawano, Wisconsin, where their descendants live today.

DIRECTIONS: From intersections of Routes 7 and 102 at the Red Lion Inn in Stockbridge Center, take Route 102 (Main Street) west 0.2 miles. The Mission House, a property of the

Trustees of Reservations, is located on the right, at the corner of Main and Sergeant streets.

In Lee, Massachusetts, local sculptor Daniel Chester French created a public drinking fountain with an image of Chief Konkapot and a fish.

Built in 1739, the house of the Reverend John Sergeant, first missionary to the Stockbridge Indians, is located on the Main Street of Stockbridge. In 1927, it was moved from its original location to Main Street, where it is known as Mission House Museum, a property of the Trustees of Reservations. Mabel Choate contracted with Fletcher Steele, a landscape architect, to work with her on the restoration of the house and the creation of period herb and flower gardens.

Mum Bett

Mum Bett, born to enslaved African parents in Claverack, New York, in the 1740s is one of the Berkshires' most famous legends. Colonel John Ashley of Sheffield, Massachusetts acquired Mum Bett and her sister when he married the daughter of her former owner. Colonel Ashley was a veteran of the French and Indian War and an early Patriot in the War for Independence.

His house in Ashley Falls, which he built in 1735 for his wife, was (and still is) the oldest in Berkshire County. It was the center of social, economic, and political life in Western Massachusetts in the Eighteenth Century.

In 1773, Colonel Ashley helped draft the famous Sheffield Declaration, a petition against British tyranny and manifesto for individual rights. Also known as the Sheffield Resolves, it was printed in The Massachusetts Spy, or, Thomas Boston Journal on February 18, 1773, three years before the Declaration of Independence was written.

Mum Bett served him and his wife, who was quick to find fault, fast to assign blame, and swift to punish. Mum Bett protected her sister, "a sickly timid creature," from the wife's anger when she could. Mum Bett served him and his wife until she was nearly forty. By then, she was known as "Mum Bett," and had a young daughter known as "Little Bett." Her husband had been killed while fighting in the Revolutionary War.

Now for our story…

Becoming Free and Equal

Before the American Revolution, slavery extended throughout the United States. In New England it was on a very limited scale. There were household slaves in Boston, who drove the coaches, cooked the dinners, and shared the luxuries of rich houses; and a few were distributed among the wealthiest of the rural population. They were not numerous enough to make the condition a great evil or embarrassment, but quite enough to show its incompatibility with the demonstration of the truth, on which our declaration of Independence is based, that "all men are born equal," and have "an inalienable right to life, liberty, and the pursuit of happiness."

Catherine Sedgewick [sic]
Slavery in New England

As part of her chores for the Ashleys, Bett served as a waitress at many of Mr. Ashley's political meetings. This task allowed her to overhear many conversations, including discussions revolving around the Bill of Rights and the new Massachusetts constitution. While serving soup or clearing the table, she began to hear words like "liberty," "justice," and "wages." Such words made her reflect on her life as a slave.

One day, her sister provoked Mrs. Ashley, which was easy to do because Mrs. Ashley had a bad temper. Walking slowly over, Mrs. Ashley grabbed a kitchen shovel hot from the oven to strike her. Mum Bett blocked her, but the shovel cut her arm to the bone. According to Catherine Sedgwick, Mum Bett later explained her hideous scar by saying, "I had a bad arm all winter, but Madam had the worst of it. I never covered the wound, and when people said to me, before Madam — 'Why Betty! What ails your arm?' I only answered — 'Ask Madam.'" Madam never again laid her hand on Lizzy.

At the time of the incident, Mum Bett left the house, refusing to return. When Colonel Ashley appealed to the law for her return, she called on Theodore Sedgwick, a friend of Colonel Ashley's and a Stockbridge lawyer with anti-slavery sentiments. All those overheard conversations paid off. She had decided that if all people were born free and equal, then the laws must apply to her, too.

Attorney Sedgwick had a daughter, Catherine, who was a novelist and prolific writer. She says in her book about Mum Bett: "She went the next day to the office of Mr. Theodore Sedgewick [sic], then in the beginning of his honourable political and legal career. 'Sire, said she, I heard that paper read yesterday, that says, All men are born equal, and that every man has a right to freedom. I am not a dumb critter; won't the law give me my freedom?' Sedgwick agreed to take the case, which was joined by another of Ashley's slaves."

Friendship with Colonel Ashley aside, Sedgwick took the case, basing it on two arguments. The first was that no Massachusetts law had ever established slavery, and that even if such a law existed, it would be annulled by the new constitution. The court agreed with Sedgwick's argument that the Massachusetts Constitution of 1780, which proclaimed that all individuals were "born free and equal" nullified the slave system. The jury found in the defendants' favor, and Mum Bett became the first enslaved African American to be freed under the Massachusetts constitution of 1780. The landmark case put Massachusetts in the forefront of the anti-slavery movement.

Ashley was ordered to pay thirty shillings and costs.

Owned by the Trustees of Reservations and listed on the National Register of Historic Places, the Ashley House exemplifies early Eighteenth Century architecture. Its Colonial period paneling, broad fireplace and staircase, hand carvings, ornaments and decorations date from the eighteenth and early nineteenth centuries.

Working for Wages

Despite pleas from Colonel Ashley that she return and work for him for wages, Mum Bett went to work for the Sedgwicks. She changed her last name to Freeman. During her tenure there, she confronted two young rebels during Shay's Rebellion. She barely had time to hide the silver in a trunk in her own room and arm herself with a heavy shovel when the men broke in, demanding to taste the Sedgwick wine. After they broke a bottle of porter in the Sedgwick cellar, she threatened them with a blow from her shovel. They changed their minds and returned to searching the house. When they reached Mum Bett's room, she sarcastically pointed out, "You'd open a poor nigger's trunk, would you, you who consider yourself so fine." Upon thinking it over, they changed their minds.

She stayed with the Sedgwick household for some time. Theodore, rose to be come a prosperous lawyer and judge who ultimately became speaker of the House. Eventually, Mum Bett set up house with her daughter, becoming a much sought-after nurse and midwife.

Mum Bett died in 1829. She is thought to have been eighty-five years old. She is the only black person to have been buried in the Stockbridge cemetery. She also is buried next to Catherine Sedgwick in the central ring of the plot reserved for the Sedgwick family.

Charles Sedgwick wrote Mom Bett's epitaph, which says, "She was born a slave and remained a slave for nearly thirty years. She could neither read nor write yet in her own sphere she had no superior or equal. She neither wasted time nor property. She never violated a trust nor failed to perform a duty. In every situation of domestic trial, she was the most efficient helper, and the tenderest friend. Good mother, farewell."

One of her great-grandchildren was W.E.B. DuBois, a civil rights activist, sociologist, and scholar. He was born almost forty years later in Great Barrington, where Attorney Sedgwick had argued the historic case.

DIRECTIONS: Colonel John Ashley House is off Route 7A in Ashley Falls, Massachusetts.

Sedgwick Pie

The Stockbridge graveyard contains the Sedgwick family burial place in one corner. It is known as the Sedgwick pie.

This view is just one slice of the Sedgwick pie.

One central high-rising stone in the center marks the grave of Judge Theodore Sedgwick, a Speaker of the House of Representatives, U.S. Senator, and a Massachusetts Supreme Court Judge. The first of the Stockbridge Sedgwicks, he was buried, with his wife Pamela next to him, in 1799. Surrounding them, facing the senior Sedgwicks, are less prominent stones, which are all the other Sedgwicks. Some of the names are almost eradicated, but they are all there — from Theodore Sedgwick, delegate to the Continental Congress and friend of George Washington, to Catherine Sedgwick, author, to Ellery Sedgwick, editor of *The Atlantic*. Supposedly, they are all buried with their heads facing out and their feet pointing in toward their ancestor.

According to Cleveland Amory (*The Last Resorts*, p. 64-65), Hon. Joseph Hodges Choate, the owner of Naumkeag, named the Sedgwick graveyard the Sedgwick pie. A well-known wit, he declared that the Sedgwicks had thought up the arrangement so that on Judgment Day when they arise and face the Judge, they wouldn't have to see anyone but Sedgwicks.

Generations have been buried in this plot, which has obviously increased substantially. During the Gilded Age, one of the Sedgwick women had a life-long attendant who asked to be buried in the plot. The family turned her down because she was not a Sedgwick. She was buried just outside, but, as time went on, she became a part of the pie.

Mum Bett was allowed in the Sedgwick pie, however. She is buried next to Catherine Sedgwick. Catherine's brother Charles, who wrote Mum Bett's epitaph, lies on Miss Sedgwick's other side.

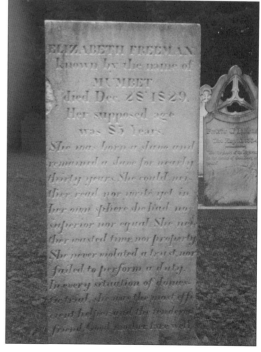

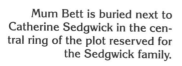

Mum Bett is buried next to Catherine Sedgwick in the central ring of the plot reserved for the Sedgwick family.

The Red Lion Inn

When the largely landless and impoverished Mohegans departed Stockbridge in 1785, they left a small rural village with dusty streets and roaming livestock. Now known as the Red Lion Inn, a stagecoach stop was established on the road that connected Boston to Albany. Travel at the time was difficult and uncomfortable, and the public house quickly became a popular stopping place for bruised and battered travelers who could stay in one of eight, low-ceiling rooms. On cool days, a fire always blazed in the hearth to welcome travelers and townspeople alike, and the innkeeper would hand them a hot punch or rum toddy. Upstairs was a large ballroom, where the big Stockbridge functions occurred. Many country dances took place there; the ladies would sip some cider; the men would indulge in something stronger.

The Red Lion Inn played a significant role in the early events in the infancy of the United States. In 1774, the County Congress or the Berkshire Convention met at Stockbridge Tavern. With Mark Hopkins and Theodore Sedgwick (See Mum Bett, p. 125) presiding, the convention members voted not to purchase any British-manufactured goods. In the winter of 1786, Daniel Shays led a group of more than one hundred armed local farmers and citizens to protest oppressive taxes. Stockbridge was chosen as headquarters for what became known as "Shays Rebellion."

Five presidents have stayed at the inn: Cleveland, Coolidge, McKinley, Theodore Roosevelt, and Franklin Roosevelt. The story is told that when President Coolidge was a candidate for Massachusetts's lieutenant governor, he was left behind at the inn on the eve of a political rally. It is said that, when found, Coolidge remarked, "I thought you would come back for me." Several of the inn's owners have been politicians.

In 1807, the "widow" Bingham sold the inn for the sum of $10,000 to Main Street storeowner Silas Pepoon. The still-present and popular Widow Bingham's Tavern commemorates her memory.

The Housatonic Railroad came to West Stockbridge in 1842 and to Stockbridge in 1850, making the region much more accessible to New Yorkers. In 1845, Samuel Gray Ward came from Boston to turn an older house into a relatively palatial structure, Highwood. It was just one of dozens of mansions, quaintly called "cottages," which were erected in the area. Writers, artists, and scholars came to the area, bringing culture and tourists with them. As the railroad grew in importance during the mid Nineteenth Century, wealthy city residents increasingly used it to escape the crowded congested urban streets during the hot summers. Enjoying the bucolic atmosphere, they reveled in the pastoral scenes and clean air of the Berkshires, either in their own summer cottages or one of the many hotels. In response to the growing popularity of the area, the Red Lion Inn expanded its facilities several times and enhanced its offerings to reflect the more cultured tastes of its guests.

Save Those Teapots

In 1873, Charles H. Plumb and his wife Mert (for whom the charming Plumb Room was named) bought the Inn and began a ninety-year family management dynasty. "Aunt Mert" was known for her sense of humor and her charming personality.

Developing her image as a voracious antique collector, Aunt Mert published a standing offer of "50 cents for a pitcher, $1 for an antique mirror." She would take a horse and buggy and scour the countryside for good antiques. She collected many of the teapots and fine antique furnishings seen in The Red Lion Inn today.

In the early 1890s, the Plumb's nephew, Allen T. Treadway, took over management of the inn. Three years later, a fire originating in the pastry kitchen could not be contained. The fire department was called.

According to the *Pittsfield Sun*, "The crowd rushed through all the rooms, rushing out the fine old furniture, bundling out all sorts of effects; confusion, haste, breakage. Fast as they worked, the Fire Fiend worked faster, biting, twisting, scorching, blistering, consuming. Nothing stayed it; nothing could kill that ravenous, raging, devouring, insatiable hunger. It drove the rescuers from place to place, advanced defiantly, seized the dear old haunts and corners, the places of rest and response, the familiar, friendly nooks and ingles – seized them though the people found and beat and deluged- seized and ruined everything so many of us loved, preyed upon everything, tyrant without mercy or conscience or remorse." Within several hours, the inn was gone.

Many of its treasured contents were saved, however. The townspeople assembled a bucket brigade. Each member of the brigade threw a bucket with one hand and grabbed a teapot with the other. Other people rushed through the building, pulling out all those lovely antiques, breaking some items in their rush, but saving many. The building burned to the ground, but many of those teapots acquired by Mrs. Plumb in the 1870s were saved.

The *Berkshire Courier* in Great Barrington reported: "Mrs. Plumb's noted collection of colonial china, pictures, wearing apparel and furniture, the largest of its kind in the country, and the delight of everyone who went to Stockbridge was saved. A few pieces were broken but in the main the collection is intact."

One of the notable pieces saved was the Lincoln Table in the center of the lobby acquired by Mrs. Plumb in the 1860s. Each Christmas, an enormous evergreen replaces it.

The owner of the inn, Mr. Treadway, undertook the restoration of the inn. In early May 1897, *The Valley Gleaner* in the nearby town of Lee announced that, "Red Lion Inn was opened to the public last Friday evening [April 30, 1897] when several out of town guests took tea and spent the night there. The Red Lion Inn never looked so handsome as it did after the entire building had been lighted up and many people were out in the streets to see the pretty sight. Just eight months from the time the old inn went up in smoke and ashes the new one was opened."

The Red Lion Inn

In November 1968, the inn was slated for destruction to make room for a gas station. John and Jane Fitzpatrick, the founders of Country Curtains, bought it, planning to use part of it as a home for Country Curtains' growing business. They became so taken with the Inn and its history that they decided to continue its operation as an inn.

The redecorated Red Lion Inn opened for year-round business in 1969. Antique furniture, china and pewter abound, and the famous teapots are on permanent display throughout the inn. Neighboring buildings were converted into guesthouses.

(Quotations from *The History of the Red Lion Inn*.)

The Red Lion Sign

From The Red Lion Inn's inception until the 1896 fire, a red lion, representing the crown, waving a green tail indicating its patriot leanings was its crest. In 1897, Mr. Treadway unveiled a new crest in the form of a shield. It had a lion; the dates 1773 and 1897, indicating the birth and rebirth of the inn; and a teapot, plate, Franklin stove, highboy, clock and two large keys, symbolizing the inn's fine collection of antiques, within the body of the shield. The traditional lion that we know today, plump and well fed, to indicate the high quality of food served at the Red Lion, replaced it in the early 1920s.

DIRECTIONS: The Red Lion Inn is located on Main Street, Stockbridge, at the corner of U.S. Route 7 and Mass. Route 102.

The Gentleman Burglar

No more fiendish punishment could be devised than that one should be turned loose in society and remain absolutely unnoticed by all the members thereof.

William James,

The Principles of Psychology

Life in the Gilded Age (1880-1920) was good for the American aristocracy. They flocked to towns like Lenox and Stockbridge to erect costly villas with beautiful vistas and extensive lawns. Natural resources, labor, production, and transportation were accessible to meet the needs of the citizens of these towns. They competed for the symbols of success: the money, the furs, the jewels, and the massive houses. Shadowbrook, the Stokes home in Lenox, with one hundred rooms, was said to be one of the largest private houses in the United States. The substantial citizens of Lenox and Stockbridge were prepared to set the standards of taste. They had servants waiting to fulfill their desires and fortunes to play with, but life could be boring.

Then in the summer of 1893, a Gentleman Burglar appeared on the scene. The talk of every fancy dinner party in town, he was a tall man with eyebrows that arched over the black or white silk handkerchief that covered the lower part of his face, and a voice that was low, and musical. He wore gloves and covered his feet; his figure was erect; and he carried himself with dignity.

Generally, this elegant burglar favored summer residents and women's boudoirs. His first expedition in Stockbridge was to the Parker cottage on Main Street, which Mrs. John Butler Swan had leased for the season. She had withdrawn a large sum from her bank. An armed guard accompanied her home, leaving his revolver with her. Her guest, Miss Stetson, and two maids were in the house that fateful evening.

Around midnight, Miss Stetson awoke to a man standing near her bed. At least six feet tall, he had a derby hat pulled far down over the forehead, a hemstitched handkerchief drawn tightly over the lower half of his face and secured behind the ears. A revolver gleamed in his right hand. She reported that his voice was positively mesmerizing. "I want your money," he said.

"I have none," replied Miss Stetson. "I only spent the night with my friend because she is afraid of you."

He picked up her rings and entered Mrs. Swan's room. She proudly informed him that she had a pistol. "Oh have you?" he said raising his arched eyebrows. To prove it to him, she removed it from beneath her pillow. After examining it, he held it to her forehead and requested the sum of money she had withdrawn from her bank. Then he carefully scrutinized her jewelry, taking it all but her mother's diamond ring.

Leaving there, he went to the David Dudley Field home. There, Mrs. Field screamed so loudly in her attempt to keep her $1,800 watch that her husband's pajama-clad valet rushed into the hall with pistol in hand. "Shoot!" she demanded, but the valet, aware of his improper attire for shooting a robber, declared, "I will, but first I must get my wrapper" and departed – quite correctly, according to that decorous Victorian society – for his robe.

The Burglar was the talk of the summer. Many female breasts quivered at the mention of his name. One reported that he was "to every inch a gentlemen." The Berkshire News declared that he should be regarded as "no ordinary or common individual but quite a refined person well advanced in the higher classes of his profession.

"He is, it would seem, a sort of pet in the village, a kind of serious night-bloomer that should be cultivated if not perpetuated. It will not be long before the cottagers of Stockbridge will, in extending invitations to their city friends, add the special inducement of his visiting the house while they are there." *(Yankee Publishing, 1974)*

Indeed, the prospect of being visited by the Gentleman Burglar was quite thrilling. Spinsters brought out their hand-made but never used trousseau nightclothes. Sheriffs honed their shooting skills. Husbands cleaned their weapons and locked all jewelry away. Streets were deserted, houses bolted and barred, and blinds drawn.

The Stockbridge ladies gave such flattering descriptions that every tall and handsome man in Stockbridge was suspect. If a man had arched eyebrows, he was a goner. One Sunday in church, Mrs. Swan noticed a tall handsome stranger with a distinctive arch to his eyebrows. She reported him, but on investigation the Sheriff found that the suspect was a Brooklyn gentleman who had just moved to Stockbridge. He left town soon after this event. The new doctor in town also became a suspect because his hands were "small and delicate" like the Burglar's.

The Burglar never worked on Sundays. He dressed like a gentleman, wore gloves, and always drove off in a buggy with fast horses. In one home he found two silver watches, but their owner claimed that they had great sentimental value. The Burglar returned the watches and left. Once he departed, the homeowner jumped on his horse and raced to town, passing the Burglar, to report the aborted crime to the Sheriff. When the Sheriff asked why the homeowner hadn't overcome him by force, the latter replied that force "would not have been in accord with the dignified manner in which affairs are conducted in Stockbridge."

The same evening (this Burglar was a busy fellow), our night visitor went to Mrs. Rosa Burns' home. Her neighbor, Mrs. Buckley swung an axe at the Burglar. The Burglar took the axe from her and used it on her rear end, which, fortunately, was well covered with a bustle. A nearby armed farmer and groom then appeared, but the Burglar diverted them by asking directions. Ever polite, those involved told him about a shortcut. Eventually, the groom and farmer gave chase, and a posse searched the countryside. They found a hidden hoard of venerable wines and imported cheese in the Crowninshield's barn. The Crowninshield's butler confirmed that the Burglar, who had sampled their champagne the night before, had absconded with these delicacies. He knew it was the Burglar because the intruder had opened a bottle of quality champagne with an obscene pop, and all Stockbridge servants knew that bubbles are wasted when the cork is popped. As the saying goes, "The ear's gain is the palate's loss." Instead, the cork should come off with a quiet sigh.

It was as if the Marx Brothers met Abbot and Costello on the streets of Stockbridge — the Burglar even robbed the Sheriff's house. When the newspapers suggested that the Burglar might be responsible for some home burglaries in the adjacent but less fashionable town of Pittsfield, Stockbridge was indignant. Their Burglar only favored the best of homes and always entered by the front door. He knew quality.

Increasingly, people were positive that he was a gentleman. Their argument was strengthened by the fact that he not only concealed his face but his hands and feet. He didn't use any skeleton key or break windows or climb on porches. He was a Gentleman Burglar.

Many elegant mansions exist in Stockbridge and Lenox.

Over games of golf, during their promenades, or at the musicales, people talked of his mesmeric voice and those delicately arched eyebrows. Those who had met him were considered fortunate and told their story again and again. Many believed that he was a professional man knowledgeable about human nature and women. Some women expressed – with some blushing – their desire to meet him after he got caught.

By the end of the season, most of the "best" people had been burglarized except for the Sedgwicks. They held their customary final dinner party with a string quartet and hand cut crystal. While they and some thirty-eight well-dressed guests were dining on the finest from the local gardens, the Burglar was selecting six bottles of fine wine, some imported cheese and bread from the pantry — and a silver knife to cut the cheese. That night he robbed six houses and returned to the Sedgwicks for a pre-dawn snack.

Stockbridge was thrilled. Their Burglar had not missed the Sedgwicks. Even the mighty could be robbed.

With everyone believing that the Burglar was an attractive gentleman, Stockbridge was dismayed to discover that he was Thomas Kinsella, a Stockbridge resident and a stonecutter employed by Joseph Choate in 1885 while building Naumkeag, his estate.

The residents who were not robbed are reported to have complained. Perhaps those who weren't robbed didn't really measure up; their diamonds were smaller, their cottages didn't have enough old masters hung on the walls. Moreover, they didn't have the story to tell. And having a good story is important in a society where one of the greatest sins is to be a bore.

Mt. Greylock

Mt. Greylock is the highest point in the purple Berkshire Hills. There you will find wild flowers blossoming two to three weeks later than in the valleys below. The snow falls earlier and lingers later than in the valley. Often the clouds and mist surround the heights when the valley is clear.

Greylock, with its sub-alpine environment, is a "monadnock," which means that it stands alone in an otherwise flat area. In the early eighteenth century, New England was a land of isolated villages, wooded hills, and uneven open fields, often divided by the traditional stonewalls. Dirt paths ran through vast expanses of deciduous woodlands to the great pine forests to the wet lowlands. With their unlimited appetite for territory and expansion, the colonists rapidly acquired land, establishing frontier communities and rules regarding law, religion, and property ownership. In theory, the colonists believed in befriending and converting the Indians to Christianity. In practice, many of the settlers wanted only to get rid of them.

The differences between the English and the native cultures increased the likelihood of friction between the colonists and the natives. The colonists assumed the Indians would adopt the English farming, shepherding, housing, legal and religious practices. The Indians resented the settlers' rules, livestock, arrogance and their relentless acquisition of land. As the settlers acquired and fenced more land, they grew more crops and raised more livestock, putting increasing pressure on Indian hunting and planting.

The Indian braves hunted and fished the land, leaving planting and other domestic tasks to their women. The land could

easily sustain the Indians because they cleared only small patch-
es. The colonists cleared, planted, and fenced the land, which
disrupted the Indian way of life. They introduced new animals,
new plants, and new diseases. The English were in the New
World to stay, and the wilderness was slowly disappearing.

Chief Greylock

Chief Greylock was born around 1660 in a Waronoke village,
which is now the town of Westfield, Massachusetts. He is said to
be a Western Abenaki Missisquoi chief of Woronoco/Pocomtuck
ancestry. Part of the Pocumtuck Confederacy of Central Massachusetts, the Waronokes were great fur trappers and hunters.
They hunted, fished, and gathered berries, nuts, and wild greens
the year around.

At this time, ownership of territories in northern New England
was in flux. The French were established in the north, calling
their region New France. The English had settled in the south
or New England and along the seaboard. The Indians, who
had lived in the region for generations, were largely overlooked,
except for their value as allies in war.

Chief Greylock is said to have lived in a secret cave on the
slopes of Mount Greylock, where he harassed the British settlers
as they moved into his domain. When war broke out between
the French and the British, Greylock and his warriors aligned
themselves with the French. He was so good at eluding the enemy that he acquired the name Wawanolet, meaning "he who
fools the others or puts someone off the track." While hunting,
his foot was crushed in a bear trap. Half his foot had to be
amputated, but it never slowed him down. He moved several
times, finally settling at Mississiquot Bay.

The Mountain

Eighteenth century English colonists called Mt. Greylock Grand Hoosuc(k). In the early nineteenth century, they called it Saddleback Mountain because of its appearance. Some time in the early nineteenth century, people began to call the mountain Greylock—maybe because of the gray clouds that clouded its peak or maybe to honor Chief Greylock.

By the mid-nineteenth century, Mt. Greylock had played host to many writers and artists, including Nathaniel Hawthorne, William Cullen Bryant, Oliver Wendell Holmes, Herman Melville, Henry David Thoreau, Daniel Chester French, and Norman Rockwell. Melville's Moby Dick is said to have been inspired by his view of the snow-covered mountain which he thought resembled the great white sperm whale's back breaking the ocean's surface. He dedicated his next novel, *Pierre*, to Mt. Greylock.

The view from Mt. Greylock.

By the late 1900s, the mountain had been almost destroyed by clear-cutting logging practices for local wood, paper, and charcoal industries. Forest fires and landslides also did their damage. A group of concerned local businessmen incorporated the Greylock Park Association (GPA) in 1885, one of the earliest land conservation groups in the state. On June 20, 1898, Greylock State Reservation was created.

In 1901, a landslide occurred on the eastern slope of the mountain. Over 1,500 feet long from top to bottom, it was called the "Chief's Steps."

In May 1990, rain fell for four days and nights causing tons of rocks, earth and trees to slide down the side of Mt. Greylock. The next morning, a giant face appeared on the eastern slope overlooking the town of Adams, Massachusetts, in Berkshire County. Most people now see the face of an old Indian Chief, or Greylock, which watches over the land he fought to preserve.

Today, the Massachusetts Department of Conservation and Recreation, Division of State Parks and Recreation, manages the 12,500-acre state reservation with approximately seventy miles of trails, including the Appalachian Trail. The Massachusetts state park system was created.

Generations later, Greylock saved the wilderness for the people.

DIRECTIONS: From Mass Pike (I-90), take Exit 2 in Lee. Follow U.S. Route 20 west to U.S. Route 7 north to Pittsfield for 11.8 miles. From downtown Pittsfield continue north on U.S. Route 7 to Lanesborough for 6.6 miles. At the brown Mount Greylock sign, turn right onto North Main Street and follow the brown lead-in signs to the park entrance; Visitor's Center is 1.5 miles from Route 7. From the Visitor's Center, the campground on Sperry Road is six miles and the summit is eight miles.

Truth or Fiction:

Going on a Lion Hunt

I often have nightmares about fierce wild beasts such as lions, tigers, and bears. I dream that they are roaring loudly in the jungle, getting my scent and sneaking up on me, chasing me, salvia dripping from their fangs… that's when I wake up screaming because I know they are going to rush in and bite my throat. But they still fascinate me. My mom says the reason I have these nightmares is because of an incident in March 1903.

When I was thirteen years old, circuses and animal shows fascinated me. I wanted to join that company of clowns, aerial artists, high wire artists, equilibrists, and the animal tamers: Mlle. Elsie and her eight prancing white stallions, Ben Snow and his leaping dogs, and Signor Arnoldo, the lion tamer. If I could join the circus, I would be happy for the rest of time or so I told myself. My ambition was to be the fearless trainer of fierce wild beasts from the jungle – just like Signor Arnoldo.

My mom said I was crazy; I should learn how to be a roofer — just like my Pop. That was a good job, she said. My Pop just puffed on his pipe, saying, "Go easy, Alice. He has his dreams." My little brother Bud would sit fascinated while I told him stories about lions and tigers and bears. Sometimes he would be the lion while I would act out Signor Arnoldo's role.

In March 1903, the F. C. Bostock Animal Show came to Pittsfield for a whole week of shows at the Academy of Music before moving east to Fitchburg. Everyone knew that F.C.

Bostock was perhaps the greatest animal trainer the world. Supposedly, he went to college and his parents thought he might become a minister, but Frank thought otherwise. When he was twelve years old, he substituted for an injured lion tamer, and that was it. Just like me, I thought. Once he came to America, he was known as "Great USA Bostock" and later "The Animal King." These days, he was too old for lion taming so Bostock hired S. Arnoldo, who was supposedly even better than he had been.

I saved up all my snow shoveling money so I could go to the show every day after school. Outside, the weather was cold and gray, with snow in grey slushy piles. But inside the Academy was a different story. On the ceiling was a maze of ropes and wires; the floor was carpeted with dirt and sawdust. The noise was overwhelming: balloon, noisemaker, and popcorn sellers shouted; elephants bellowed; lions and tigers roared; monkeys screamed; and horses neighed. The Academy reeked of sawdust, tobacco, popcorn, manure, and gunpowder. And the assembly of people was amazing: farmers, spangled trapeze walkers, women in shirtwaists and wool or serge suits, whip-snapping beast tamers, men in cutaway frock coats and top hats, harem girls with bare midriffs and glittering jeweled appliqués, and young men, who should have been looking for jobs, according to my Pop. I think he was trying to give me a hint.

Each day I watched Miss Miranda and her horse Cowboy work through a precise military drill. Her horse could do most everything except stand on its head. Clad in a scanty spangled outfit, she and Cowboy would sail through a flaming hoop. At the end of her act, he would practically be walking on his hind legs, while she would wave happily at the audience. Mom didn't like it that we saw most of her legs. The sad-eyed clowns would ride horses, donkeys, and zebras. They would somersault, fight, tumble, and allow themselves to be chased, kicked, and butted. The shiny seals balanced balls on their noses, snapped up buckets of fish, and played unrecognizable tunes on their horns. Signor Arnoldo, sitting cross-legged upon the forehead of India, the biggest elephant, always led the six other elephants in the thundering grand finale. My friend Ben and I could almost reach out and touch their quivering flanks before they reared up on their hind legs to trumpet farewell.

Blonde Madame Barlowe worked the lions in the afternoon show. As gaudy red lights played on a circular cage and the drums thudded, she would arm herself with whip, chair and blank-loaded revolver before she stepped into the cage. Then she would put the four lions through their paces. The lions snarled and hissed and didn't look like they enjoyed themselves, but they did what she commanded until that fateful Saturday.

At the Saturday matinee, we were all watching – hearts in our throats – when Madame Barlowe stepped into the cage where four large lionesses were pacing back and forth. The one known as Victoria was a young, six hundred pound lioness, who always appeared angry. She snarled, whined, and paced the cage with her tail swishing angrily.

By the end of the week, Ben and I knew Madame Barlowe's lion routine by heart. A good deal of the routine was spent with her posing and swinging her long blond hair around while the lions posed on their pedestals. She also had them climbing a ladder and walking across a plank in mid air. That Saturday three lionesses did it perfectly. Victoria just sat there sullenly. Madame Barlowe used the whip, but Victoria still ignored her, snapping and snarling. When Madame Barlowe approached her, she crouched, with her tail snapping back and forth, like she was going to jump on her. Finally, Madame Barlowe fired her pistol, and Victoria went and sulked on her pedestal, growling. She looked just like my little brother, Bud, when Mom said he couldn't have dessert.

At the end of the show, the ringmaster, resplendent in black top hat, red cutaway, white riding breeches, silvered-flowered vest, and black top hat, announced, "Last show is tonight. See you then or next year." Before I went home, I went to visit the lions one last time, wondering when my parents would let me join the circus. While I was hanging around, I heard Madame Barlowe tell William Crawford, the evening animal trainer, that Victoria was being difficult. I wondered what he could do, but I had to get home before Mom yelled at me for being late.

Later I heard that when Crawford entered the cage to feed the lions their horsemeat dinner, Victoria was still growling. Ignoring her, he turned his back, a huge mistake. She lunged at him, ripping his chin open with one of her long claws. Knocking him up against the cage bars, she took hold of his shoulder with her jaws. Although Crawford's wounds were bleeding severely, he grabbed a pike pole and pushed it at her. Snarling, she backed into a corner, and he escaped the cage.

The doctors cauterized his wounds to prevent jungle fever and gangrene and then stitched him up. His arm in a sling and his face the color of chalk, Crawford returned to the Academy for the night's performance. Before the performance, he met with the stagehands. He warned them, "Watch Victoria every second tonight. She's tasted blood–my blood–and she might want more. But don't shoot unless you have to. She's very valuable."

The stagehands kept a close eye on Victoria, but nothing happened. She paced right and left on his command. She posed on her pedestal and even walked the plank when he demanded it. Crawford, like Arnoldo, had the almost telepathic knack of making his beasts understand what he wants.

After the show, the stagehands began to pair the animals up and load them into their traveling cages. With two animals to a cage, the cage weighed about 1,300 pounds. Usually, they used a block and tackle to hoist all theatrical equipment and scenery from the wagons in the courtyard at the rear of the Academy to the third floor stage. This time, however, the Academy manager forbade the stagehands to hoist the animals in their heavy wooden cages. Instead, when the show came to Pittsfield, the stagehands lugged the heavy animal cages up the fire escape and onto the stage.

That Saturday night it began to rain, which made the task of moving the animals down the fire escape much too difficult. So a crew of carpenters rigged up a big beam that projected out from the upper story stage entrance. From that, they hung a block and tackle so the cages could be lowered onto the wagons below.

After they had lowered the scenery, baggage, and props, the stagehands began lowering the cages. Panthers, jaguars, and a big black Nubian lion were carefully loaded into the waiting wagons. The next to be loaded was the cage containing the two lions, Victoria and Sappho. On the ground, two horse-drawn wagons were standing ready to be loaded. A crowd of spectators watched the cage containing the two lions as it swung out from the third story and was slowly lowered to the waiting wagons.

When it was about two thirds the way down, the rope broke. The cage crashed to the ground. The top flew off with a bang, and both lionesses leaped out into the crowd. They tell me that the people watching the loading really ran. The Monday edition of the *Berkshire Eagle* said, "As some of those spectators haven't been seen since Saturday night, it is presumed they are still running."

At first, both lionesses appeared stunned. Then Victoria rose up and sprang for the horse on the smaller wagon. With a great roar that could be heard for miles, she lunged for the horse's throat and dragged him to the ground. She shook him like a cat shakes a mouse. At the same time, Sappho leaped for the two horses harnessed to the other larger wagon. Snorting and kicking, the horses tried to escape, but she bared her teeth and pulled one screaming horse down. People said they heard a dry snapping noise like bones being broken. Signor Arnoldo began to shoot in the air, hoping to frighten the lions away from the horses. Victoria crawled under the express wagon.

Signor Arnoldo crept forward with his gun. When he was in range of Victoria, he fired directly at her. She came leaping out, and then dropped dead. What a shame. Lions are so valuable.

Meanwhile, Sappho, like any exploring cat, wandered out of the courtyard and on to Cottage Row, where she just meandered on down the sidewalk. Later almost everyone in town swore they had seen her that night.

Although the fearful crowd had initially scurried for shelter, they must have awakened everyone in town. People got up, got dressed, and ran out to chase the lionesses. Ben came and told us, and Pop and I went out with him. My mother was having a conniption, waving her hands, and crying, but Pop said we would be all right. We were just going on a lion hunt.

A policeman told us we should head for safety, but we had a big stick and my BB gun, so we walked about poking into hedges, under cellars and wagons, and anywhere that we thought a lion could hide. Just where would those lions appear? Just what or who would they eat while they were in town.

It was foggy that night. Mr. and Mrs. McCarty were coming home from the store, where he had bought a ten pound rib roast for Sunday dinner, when they saw what they thought was Henry Piper's big dog, Prince, standing right in the middle of the sidewalk. Mr. McCarty has a bad habit of talking in baby talk. Supposedly, he said something like "Hello Princey, Whincey. How's the old doggie woggie tonight?" Sitting back on its haunches, the huge animal licked at its chops and swiped at Mr. McCarty. Luckily, for Mr. McCarty, he missed.

Mrs. McCarty could not believe Prince's bad manners. Putting down her basket, she marched right up to Sappho, rebuking him. "Bad dog, Prince. Now get out of our way. Go on home. Now."

When the lioness bared her sharp white fangs and didn't budge, Mrs. McCarty lifted her umbrella and smacked the beast right on top of its head. With an astounded yelp, the animal leaped over the hedge and disappeared into the night. Later, Mrs. McCarty told my mother that she was really surprised when she read the headline in the Sunday newspaper: "Escape from Circus. Pittsfield Citizens Have Narrow Escapes. Enraged Beasts Kill One Horse – Injure Others - Hundreds Flee as Lions Roam Streets." From then on, people always said – with total awe – "Mrs. McCarty, a REALLY BRAVE woman."

All that night people who didn't know about the escaped lion brushed up against what they thought was a shaggy dog while the searchers were poking and prodding under bushes, wagons, and cellar holes and looking with alarm at the big trees. What if she climbed one of those? Would she leap on us? Sink her sharp fangs into our necks?

Pop, Ben, and I wandered around town for a long time, but Sappho seemed to be frequenting a deeply forested area.

Finally, people said they had seen her trotting across the North Street Bridge. When we reached there, she disappeared behind a vine-covered lattice near the Central Garage. Nobody could tell where she was hiding that dark night. Of course, I had to throw a rock into the bush once or maybe it was twice, and the sudden burst of sound made everyone scream and run out of the way. Then they would come back, acting like they hadn't run, and suggesting such things as "Build a fire." "Send for the militia." Pop whispered to me, "Lions are never tame, it takes strategies to deal with that."

Finally, the night watchman opened the side door to the garage and Sappho went inside. When the door closed, everyone shouted. Now all we had to do was to take her to the train.

We could hear a great commotion inside the garage. It turned out that Sappho bit into a tire, which exploded with a bang. Terrified, she leapt over the cars and ran around the garage, making a large mess.

Signor Arnoldo stepped inside. If anyone could calm Sappho down, he could. All the lions knew he was the boss. The stagehands had gone back to the theater and grabbed a cage, which they placed against the sliding door. We could hear Signor Arnoldo talking to Sappho just as my mother talks to me sometimes when I've been bad. He calmed her right down and led her to the cage. In she went — glad to be in her home again. All that night she wailed and moaned for Victoria. Suddenly, she didn't seem like a super predator anymore — she had feelings just like I did.

Victoria was skinned, and a taxidermist bought her hide, although souvenir hunters had spoiled it. We all wanted a memento of that exciting lion hunt. To this day, I still have one sharp tooth.

Bibliography

Abbott, Katharine. *Old Paths and Legends of the New England Borders*. New York, New York: G.P. Putnam's Sons, 1907.

Amory, Cleveland. *The Last Resorts*. New York, New York: Harper & Brothers, 1952.

Byron, Carl R. *A Pinprick of Light*. Brattleboro, Vermont: The Stephen Greene Press, 1974.

Chapman, Gerard. *The Gentleman Burglar and Other Favorites*. Great Barrington, Massachusetts: Attic Revivals Press, 1994.

Jackson, Richard S. Jr. and Cornelia Brooke Gilder. *Houses of the Berkshires 1870-1930*. New York, New York: Acanthus Press, 2006.

Owens, Carole. *The Berkshire Cottages: A Vanishing Era*. Stockridge, Massachusetts: Cottage Press, Inc. 1984.

Peattie, Roderick, Ed. *The Berkshires: the Purple Hills*. New York, New York: The Vanguard Press, Inc., 1948.

Perry, Clay. *New England's Buried Treasure*. New York, New York: Stephen Daye Press, 1946.

Red Lion Inn. *A History of the Red Lion Inn*. Stockbridge, Massachusetts: Red Lion Inn, 1987.

Schultz, Eric B and Michael Tougias. *King Philip's War*. Woodstock, Vermont: The Countrymen Press, 1999.

Sedgwick, Sarah Cabot and Christina Sedgwick Marquand. *Stockbridge 1739-1939*. Great Barrington, Massachusetts: The Berkshire Courier, 1939.

Skinner, Charles M. *Myths and Legends of Our Own Land — Volume 04: Tales of Puritan Land*. Philadelphia, Pennsylvania: Lippincott Publishing Co., 2006.

Smith, Charles and Susan Smith. *Discover the Berkshires*. Guilford, Connecticut: The Globe Pequot Press, 2003.

Todd, Charles Burr. *In Olde Massachusetts*. New York, New York: The Grafton Press, 1971.

Vaughan, Alden T. Ed. *New England Encounters: Indians and Euro Americans ca. 1600-1850*. Boston, Massachusetts: Northeastern University Press, 1999.

Vaughan, Alden T. and Edward W. Clark. *Puritans Among the Indians*. Cambridge, Massachusetts: The Belknap Press, 1981.

Williams, John. *The Redeemed Captive Returning to Zion*. Ann Arbor, Michigan: University Microfilms, Inc. 1966.

Yankee Magazine Staff. *Danger, Disaster, and Horrid Deeds*. Dublin, New Hampshire, 1974.

Articles and Internet

"A Wild Man of the Mountains: Two Young Vermont Hunters Terribly Scared."

Christian History Institute. "John Sergeant and the Stockbridge Indians 1999-2006."

Damon-Bach, Lucinda. "Slavery in New England by Miss Sedgewick." English Department at Salem State College - ©2002.

Durwin, Joe. "Bizarre Berkshires: Tales Spooky and Otherwise," 2004.

Durwin, Joe. "These Mysterious Hills," 2006

Egleston, N.H. "Story of the Hoosic Tunnel." *The Atlantic Monthly* Vol. XLIX, 1882.

New York Times (1857-Current file). New York, New York: Oct 18, 1879, p. 1

Hanny, Carol. "Megaliths, caves and other interesting stuff!" Internet site

Howes, Marc. "The History of the Hoosac Tunnel." 2004 Internet

"In Tanglewood's Tent." *Time Magazine*, August 16, 1937.

"Model for the Frontier." *Time Magazine*, July 4, 1969.

"Plumb's Hotel, in Stockbridge, Destroyed by Fire." *Pittsfield Sun*, (MA) September 3, 1896, p. 2

Smith, Gary. Compiler, "Finding Aid for the Hoosac Tunnel Collection," at The North Adams Public Library, North Adams, Massachusetts, 01247. May 2003. Internet

Index